The
Master
Potter

REVISED EDITION

Nwabuogo N. B. Okafo

The Master Potter
First published in 2011, Revised edition 2019

Copyright © Nwabuogo N.B. Okafo
A Publication of Kingdom Ambassadors Ministries.
E-mail: ogofavor13@gmail.com

ISBN: 978-1-7346481-0-2 (Print)
        978-1-7346481-1-9 (E-book)

Printed in the United States of America

Dedication

This book is passionately dedicated to all lovers of God, the saints combatant. Great peace have those who love the law of the Lord; nothing can cause them to stumble (Psalm 119:165). You will not end in shame!

"All scripture is given by inspiration of God, and is profitable for doctrine, for reproof, for correction, for instruction in righteousness: that the man of God may be perfect, thoroughly furnished unto all good works."
(2 Timothy 3:16–17)

"So I went down to the potter's house, and I saw him working at the wheel. But the pot he was shaping from the clay was marred in his hands; so the potter formed it into another pot, shaping it as seemed best to him. Then the word of the Lord came to me. He said, "Can I not do with you, Israel, as this potter does?" declares the Lord. "Like clay in the hand of the potter, so are you in my hand, Israel." *(Jeremiah 18:3-6 NIV)*

Acknowledgments

To God Almighty, who gave the inspiration for this work and patiently waited for my compliance.

To my sweetheart and ministry partner, Onyeka, who God uses to strengthen my weaknesses. I appreciate his love, understanding, unequalled support and devotion.

To the late Dr. Chioma Uzoho, for the enthusiasm, thoroughness and fervent love which inspired her thoughtful contributions and editing of this work.

To Rev Can. Levi Anyikwa, a brother and bosom friend, for his sacrificial love and contributions to make this work a masterpiece.

To Pastors Emma and Oluchukwu David for your invaluable contributions.

Many thanks to you all.

Contents

Introduction

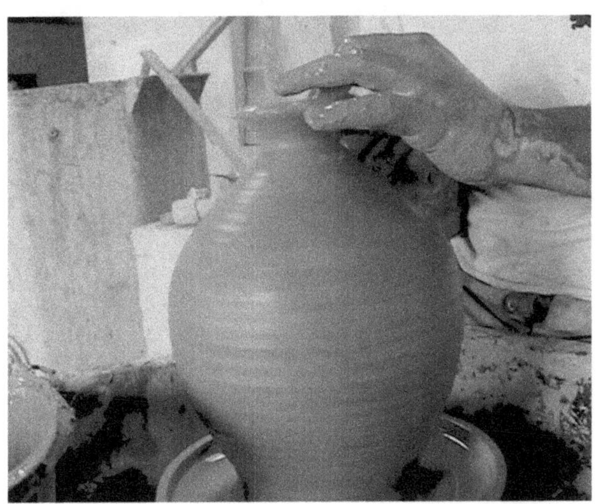

Introduction

There is hardly any Christian who has not read the illustration God made to Jeremiah the prophet concerning the potter and the clay. But how many people truly understand the lesson God is trying to convey through that illustration? Though it is a very popular scriptural quotation, which many preachers and songwriters have expressed verbally and on paper, it cannot be deeply understood just through reading and singing. It is a practical lesson and requires the kind of practical steps Jeremiah took: observing the potter at work and possibly interacting with him, as well as asking some questions and obtaining the answers. Perhaps using this same approach can help us understand the lesson the Lord, who is the Master Potter, is trying to drive home. It is not easy for everyone, hence the writing of this little book. This book is meant to help those who may not have the convenience of visiting a potter or a potter's workshop. It is also meant for those people who, though they have visited a potter at work, may not truly understand his material (clay) and his activities.

There is a relationship, an intimacy, which led to the appointment God gave Jeremiah at the potter's house. It is a kind of intimacy that every Christian should cultivate if we are to discover and fulfill God's purpose for our lives. It is this place of meditation and prayer in which God would often relay His messages. There is a need, therefore, for us to prioritize the presence of God and abide there, in order to hear His voice, and receive His teaching, revelation, and guidance. Lessons and revelations obtained firsthand in this way can hardly be forgotten and they have far-reaching effects on the life of every believer.

Knowing we are clay is basic, in the same way that we acknowledge we are human, but knowing that does not help us much in being who He wants us to be and attaining to those attributes He is teaching us in this lesson. Sadly, this is the place many Christians and preachers stop, as far as the understanding of this Scripture is concerned. It is not enough to be saying or singing, "You are the Potter, and I am the clay." We must really understand what that means. We need to know the qualities of good clay because not all clay is workable, or easy to use. Good clay must be alive and responsive. It can be very frustrating to work with gritty, non-plastic clay. Clay must be processed before it can be effectively used. Most of the experiences we pass through as believers are meant to be part of our preparation to make us fit for God's use.

Naturally, clay is not attractive and may not be useful for any purpose. The potter is the one who identifies its potential and makes an aesthetic utilitarian vessel out of it. Even when the pot he is making gets marred, the potter is able to redesign and make a beautiful pot out of it. In the same way, our mistakes do not spell eternal doom. Instead God beckons us to repent, turn our backs to the past, and yield ourselves to His creative work. Though we fall, the Lord is able to raise us up again.

The work of a potter with clay is all about purifying and giving it a purpose. A potter makes something meaningful out of the ordinary and mundane; it's about taking something that's ugly and making it attractive. The Lord is in the business of beautifying lives, but for those lives to be transformed, they must be yielded to Him in absolute surrender, just like workable clay yields itself to the potter.

THE APPOINTMENT

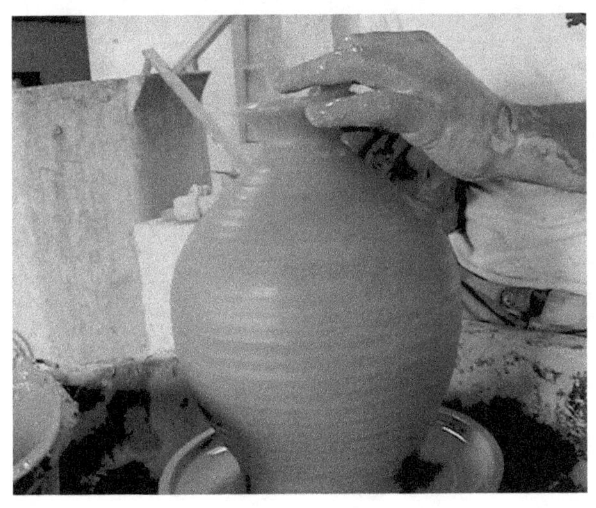

THE APPOINTMENT

**This is the word that came to Jeremiah from the Lord: "Go down to the potter's house, and there I will give you my message."
—Jeremiah 18:1–2 NIV**

Background: The book of Jeremiah was originally written with the people of Judah in mind. Judah was also known as the southern kingdom with Jerusalem as its capital. The nation was quickly turning away from God—sliding towards destruction. Jeremiah urged God's people to repent of their sins and return to God.

By human standards, Jeremiah was a failure. He served as God's oracle to Judah, but the people never paid attention to his message because he was poor and not a person of note in their eyes. He was persecuted repeatedly for faithfully proclaiming God's message. At one time, he was thrown into prison. At another time, he was cast into a dry well, and forcibly taken to Egypt. Jeremiah was mostly alone, especially since his messages were negative. He didn't prophesy what his audience liked to hear. He was unpopular in his own time, and is called "the weeping prophet" because he wept over what he saw would befall his people.

In God's eyes however, Jeremiah was very successful because of his obedience and faithfulness to the call of God, in spite of the opposition he faced from those around him. He was a man of God's presence. It is no wonder he was God's oracle to his generation, even though they did not pay attention to his message. Nevertheless, his prophecies were fulfilled with Babylon eventually conquering Judah in 586 BC, while the prophecies of those who prophesied good at the time came to nothing.

> And if thou say in thine heart, how shall we know the word which the Lord hath not spoken? When a prophet speaketh in the name of the Lord, if the thing follow not, nor come to pass, that is the thing which the Lord hath not spoken, but the prophet hath spoken it presumptuously: thou shalt not be afraid of him. *(Deuteronomy 18:21-22)*

God is a righteous, wise, and loving father. He is Lord over all. And He brings events to pass according to *His* timing, not ours (Ecclesiastes 3:11). When we submissively follow His plans, we have an enduring relationship with Him and enjoy a fulfilled life.

The Lord summoned Jeremiah the prophet to a meeting with Him at the potter's house. It was a private, classified, exclusive, and intimate invitation. This was an urgent and critical message which God could not afford to deliver to Jeremiah amidst the noise and chaos of family and societal distractions. It was a practical session, hence the choice of a potter's workshop. In the same way, the Lord is inviting you, the reader, to an exclusive time of interaction with Him today. It is a call to a private, meditative, and life-transforming lesson. First, God called Jeremiah to get his attention. This required that Jeremiah be available. God is always looking for available vessels, not necessarily *big or powerful* ones, but willing and available ones. Obedience to this call will lead to the next step:

"And there I will give you my message."
(Jeremiah 18:2b NIV)

This invitation requires an urgent and obedient response today too, as modelled by Jeremiah. He immediately set out to the potter's house to hear this all-important message from God. Only prompt obedience will bring about the message. Had Jeremiah delayed, he probably would not have met the potter at work, nor heard the message from the Lord. *Any man or woman who must carry out serious business with the Lord must avoid a lifestyle of procrastination.*

Only prompt obedience will bring about the message.

Many activities compete for our attention today, ranging from secular or religious to family issues. We often find ourselves struggling and sometimes unable to meet our daily schedule. The danger is that we have very little or no time at all to pay attention to God. Personal devotion (our quiet time with the Lord) is lacking in the lives of many believers today. Even those who manage to observe it struggle with maintaining the self-discipline required to concentrate and practice this important discipline. Because of this, many of the Lord's messages are undelivered, misunderstood, or not understood at all. It is not surprising that God He invited Jeremiah to a time away, a time of meditation. You may even call it a kind of retreat, an interruption to Jeremiah's busy schedule. A time of divine teaching using practical life experience—pot making.

How can a Christian maintain a life of personal devotion in the face of modern-day challenges? I have heard people complain that twenty-four hours is not enough time to get everything done that is required in one day. They think it should have been thirty-six hours or more. By this, they imply that they cannot do all the things they need to do in one day. Often, they find themselves too busy. They live lives enthralled to a congested and out-of-control schedule, and everything on it is considered equally important. Every activity must be accomplished, and there is no prioritizing. We all get caught up in this. In the end, we live painful lives, and do nothing thoroughly. We are jacks of all trade, and masters of none. This is not the will of the Lord for any of us. All mankind has been given twenty-four hours a day—men and women, young and old, the successful and the failure, the poor and the rich. What you do with your time determines how you live; and how you live determines how you end up: happy or sad, fulfilled or unfulfilled, victorious or defeated, poor or rich.

We often wake with our heads crammed with the things we must do. If intentional care is not taken, we might not pray before jumping into action, without seeking the face of the Lord for guidance or appreciating Him for the grace He has given us to see another day in the land of the living. A woman, for instance, wakes up with the thoughts: "What am I going to fix for breakfast? What do I have available and what do I need to pick up from the store? I have to start baking this and that before I start my morning devotion. Oh, my, I forgot that! What do I need to get ready for lunch? What do I need to get ready for dinner? I can start the laundry too, and while the machine is running, I will start praying. Yes, that's a good idea"

It is good to multitask in order to save time, but too often, if we begin like this in the kitchen, we might end up getting so ensconced in what must be done that we never get to that time with Jesus. There are just too many chores in that kitchen vying for our attention. Even if we eventually sit down and seek the Lord, by then our day has already been split into two, and we find ourselves utilizing only half of the time we would have normally spent in God's presence to start our day. On top of that, the quality of our communion with God is affected because we are now struggling to focus. Our mind is partly connected to the food we are preparing, and the laundry we have already begun. We labor to get everything perfectly done at the same time, but it doesn't always follow that way. Jesus said to Martha in Luke 10:

> "But one thing is needful: and Mary hath chosen
> that good part, which shall not be taken from her."
> *(Luke 10:42)*

In this verse, our Lord Jesus Christ Himself shows that we must carefully choose what is more important. He commended Mary because she chose the spiritual before the physical. We don't have to be torn between activities, and live our lives doing everything haphazardly. The truth is that what we receive from our communion with God cannot be taken away from us: wisdom, peace, direction, favor, and all we need to succeed for the rest of the day. David said in Psalm 5:

> My voice shalt thou hear in the morning, O Lord; in
> the morning will I direct my prayer unto thee, and
> will look up. *(Psalm 5:3)*

> In the morning, O Lord, you will hear my voice; in
> the morning I will prepare [a prayer and a sacrifice]
> for You and watch and wait [for You to speak to my
> heart]. *(Psalm 5:3 AMP)*

This must be one of the reasons David is called "a man after God's own heart." David had an intimate relationship with God. He was so close to God that nothing could cut him off from his "early morning sacrifice" (his time of personal devotion with God). If any man or woman wants to be a special vessel in the hand of God, he or she must be a man or woman of covenant sacrifice. We must give priority to His presence, disciplining ourselves to abide in God's presence. To do this, it is vital that we start our day with the Lord and continue with Him all day.

> ## The time we spend in the presence of God determines the power we carry.

The time we spend in the presence of God determines the power we carry. No man or woman of God is made in public. According to Dr. Paul Enenche, a Nigerian pastor, the seed of life is time.[1] God has given man seed, so that he can face the future without fear, as long as man applies that seed appropriately. Dr. Enenche explained that the best way to spend time is in four ways:

First and foremost, we seek Him and have regular times of intimacy with God. By this we gain a sense of His presence with us and life's provision as a result. Matthew 6 says:

> But seek ye first the kingdom of God, and his righteousness; and all these things shall be added unto you. *(Matthew 6:33)*

---

1. Dr. Paul Enenche is the senior pastor of Dunamis International Church, in Abuja, Nigeria.

To spend time in God's presence is to invest in the harvest of pleasure in life. He fills our hearts with his joy, no matter what life throws at us. Psalm 16 says:

> Thou wilt shew me the path of life: in thy presence
> is fulness of joy; at thy right hand there are pleasures
> for evermore. *(Psalm 16:11)*

He sets our feet on the path of doing service for Him in soul winning. When we are abiding in Him, winning others to Him comes naturally. The man that spends time harvesting souls is rewarded by God. He is placed on God's payroll (John 4:5).

Another reward is personal development. This can take the form of academic pursuits, reading, training, seminars, and conferences. God will lead us into the best development plan for each of us, so we will grow in the way He has planned.

Remember that in Psalm 5, David wrote, "I will prepare for you and watch and wait" (Psalm 5:3 AMP). David woke up every day expecting the usual early morning appointment with the Lord. In David's time with God, he showered praises on the Lord, laid down his burdens, and waited for His word (direction). It is no wonder that David never lost a battle in his life. No matter how hard the enemy pressed, David sought the Lord and received direction from God before he went into any battle.

> And David was greatly distressed; for the people
> spake of stoning him, because the soul of all the
> people was grieved, every man for his sons and
> for his daughters: but David encouraged himself in
> the Lord his God. And David said to Abiathar the
> priest, Ahimelech's son, I pray thee, bring me hither
> the ephod. And Abiathar brought thither the ephod
> to David. And David enquired at the Lord, saying,

Shall I pursue after this troop? shall I overtake them? And he answered him, Pursue: for thou shalt surely overtake them, and without fail recover all. *(1 Samuel 30:6-8)*

David was unlike Saul, Israel's first king and his master, who usually moved ahead of the Lord, following his own path. Here is an example of Saul's choices:

And Saul went on this side of the mountain, and David and his men on that side of the mountain: and David made haste to get away for fear of Saul; for Saul and his men compassed David and his men round about to take them. But there came a messenger unto Saul, saying, Haste thee, and come; for the Philistines have invaded the land. Wherefore Saul returned from pursuing after David, and went against the Philistines: therefore they called that place Selahammahlekoth. *(1 Samuel 23:26-28)*

Tragically, Saul ended up committing suicide.

Then said Saul unto his armourbearer, Draw thy sword, and thrust me through therewith; lest these uncircumcised come and thrust me through, and abuse me. But his armourbearer would not; for he was sore afraid. Therefore Saul took a sword, and fell upon it. *(1 Samuel 31:4)*

What a miserable end!

Child of God, do you take the time to seek the Lord for direction? Have you ever heard the Lord speak to you? Do you pursue His will concerning your life, family, and ministry?

Or do you move and expect Him to follow? Do you start your projects your way, and ask Him to bless them later? Are you living according to your will or His? You might be doing His work, but did you take the time to find out whether what you are doing is what He wants you to do, done in the manner He desires? Sometimes we get distracted from our real purpose with good things, like fellowship and church activities. We fail to recognize that these "good things" can be another strategy of the Devil to keep us away from what is more important: our own personal communion with God.

Are you living according to your will or His?

Evangelist Andrew Wommack shared an experience he had as an American soldier in Vietnam. He spent several hours every day studying the Scripture and enjoying the fellowship of the Holy Spirit. He was flourishing spiritually. At the same time, he longed for the time when he would return home and enjoy the fellowship of the brethren at his church again. He felt he was missing a lot in not being involved in the activities back home. When he got home, he was reunited with his church and immediately became immersed in their activities. He was happy to be home and busy with church activities once again—which is what he had prayed for. However, it wasn't long before he noticed that he was no longer experiencing the presence of God as he had before. God didn't seem to be near him as He used to be. Instead of flourishing spiritually, his spiritual life seemed to be spiraling downward. He prayed, asking God why this was happening. God's answer was as unexpected as it was honest: The Lord told him that he had become *too busy for Him!* How could that be? He was doing God's work every day! The Lord told him that many of the activities in the church were used to tie Christians down; and they actually weakened them spiritually. He repented and retraced his steps, focusing once again on spending time in the Word and having real communion with God. As a result, he was restored.

The Lord told him that he had become *too busy for Him*!

As a young Christian, I was taught that if I wanted to be effective as a Christian, I should not be in more than two fellowship groups at a time. But as time went on, I veered away from this wise counsel. My family always belonged to one denomination, and we were very active in it. Any church we attended found ways to keep us occupied with service, utilizing our gifts and commitment. Oftentimes, we were interested in some non-denominational Christian groups too, due to our hunger for more of the Word and our desire to meet broader social demands. My husband had a preferred group, which the entire family attended. I also had a women's intercessory group which I was called to by God. Of course, my family joined me too. We were committed to each group in varying degrees. The result was that we found ourselves running from pillar to post, especially on Sundays with hardly enough time to meditate on what we had gleaned from each of those meetings as they went by each week. To make matters worse, each group also had midweek activities. Over time, all this became time-consuming and draining, both physically and financially. I whined and complained, but we couldn't reach an agreement about where to focus. I prayed earnestly for God's help. Finally, with sober reflection, I realized that God had called me specifically to one group, and that was the women's intercessory group. It was friends and family that had called me into the other two ministries. God is not an author of confusion. He has a given location for each one of His children. If you seek Him, He will make that clear to you. If man called you, you could expect your reward from him. As long as I was comfortable with running from fellowship to fellowship, God allowed me to do that; but as soon as I became uncomfortable with that (because I knew something was wrong with the excessive activities I was involved in), He took me back to the last time He spoke to me. If you are expecting to receive direction and it is not immediately forthcoming, think about the last time you heard from Him. It is not likely that He is going to tell you anything different from what you have heard from Him originally on a particular issue. He has a specific plan for each of us, and will faithfully lead us into it.

> He has a given location for each one of His children. If you seek Him, He will make that clear to you.

In time I began to focus on which ministry God specifically desired me to serve in, my own location. Today, I am happier and more fulfilled doing what He wants me to do. It is time to prayerfully seek God and know your calling. Friends and brethren may not be happy with your decision, but you must judge for yourself whether it is better to obey men rather than God. If your goal is to please men, you run the risk of displeasing God and losing everything in the end. If you decide to flow with the crowd, you stand the risk of missing out on God's purpose for your life. Remember this: When you stand before God at the end of your journey, you stand alone. We must all face Him to give account of our lives, ministry, talents, time, and money—and whatever else God has given us for His kingdom. Jesus said to Martha:

> "Martha, Martha," the Lord answered, "you are worried and upset about many things, but few things are needed–or indeed only one. Mary has chosen what is better, and it will not be taken away from her." *(Luke 10:41-42 NIV)*

The *NIV Life Application Study Bible* contains this comment regarding this passage: "Mary and Martha both loved Jesus. On this occasion they were both serving Him. But Martha thought Mary's style of serving was inferior to hers. She didn't realize that in her desire to serve, she was actually neglecting her guest. Are you so busy doing things for Jesus that you're not spending any time with Him? Don't let your service become self-serving. Jesus did not blame Martha for being concerned about household chores. He was only asking her to set priorities right. Service to Christ can degenerate into mere busywork that is no longer full of devotion to God."[2]

> **If you decide to flow with the crowd, you stand the risk of missing out on God's purpose for your life.**

This is where the problem lies. It's not the issue of being active for God, your church, or fellowship. Does

---

2. *Life Application Study Bible: New International Version.* 2017. Carol Stream, IL: Tyndale House Publishers.

your service involve devotion to God? Or does it take you further away from Him? Does it leave you with no time for personal worship, prayers, and Bible study? It's time for self-evaluation. It's time to tell yourself the truth. If your activities are leaving you empty and without quality time for personal development, then it's time to make some serious decisions and cut off those things that are keeping you out of God's presence. Finishing well requires purpose and discipline. This demands building the will to say no to some habits and activities: this is the heart of self-discipline. It might mean saying no to some friends and activities that lead you away from God or keep you too occupied or too tired to have time for those truly essential disciplines of the Christian life: worship, prayer, and Bible study.

> ## Finishing well requires purpose and discipline.

Are you where God wants you to be right now? Maybe He just needs your attention. Perhaps you simply need to be still before Him to receive divine direction. How can you do that if you are too busy with fellowship or church activities in His service? You might be laboring in another man's vineyard! You might be sincere about what you are doing, but sincerely wrong. Take some time to seek Him and make sure you are where He wants you to be, and doing what He wants you to do. Some people say, "I can't hear God," or "He does not speak to me," or "I don't have the gift of hearing God." There's no such thing as a "gift of hearing" your Father! He says this:

You will seek me and find me when you seek me with all your heart. *(Jeremiah 29:13 NIV)*

"My sheep hear my voice, and I know them, and they follow me" *(John 10:27)*

If you are one of His sheep, you will hear Him.

How can you do that if you are too busy with fellowship or church activities in His service?

God is constantly speaking. You may just have a *receiving* problem. It might be that you don't understand His voice, but that problem will be solved as you spend time with Him in prayer and meditation. It is through these two disciplines that we get accustomed to His voice. You may not be able to hear Him when you are too busy. God wants to spend time with you and speak to you personally. Don't be the kind of Christian that is comfortable with secondhand messages. Seek to hear your Father for yourself. This will happen when you value His presence. Don't settle for anything less. Don't spend your time and resources on that which does not profit you.

Desire is a very important key to receiving or hearing from God. Let Him know you will not move until you hear Him. If you are impatient and only going to give Him a few minutes to speak before you make your own decisions, you may never hear Him. Ask for His leading before you make any decision, and *wait expectantly.*

God spoke to Abraham in the cool of the day. It was quiet and peaceful at that time. It is very difficult to receive from God when we are physically noisy, buying and selling, talking and planning, and doing our thing. Jesus spoke about this in Luke 17:27. There should be moderation to our activities, whether they are religious or secular. Sometimes we are not caught up in God's business or church activities. Instead, we are engrossed in the pursuit of material things and money to the extent that we have little or no time at all for God. Some of us work multiple jobs, so that we can accomplish self-set goals. The more we get, the more we want to get. We work seven days a week with little time for God, family, and the things of life that really matter. Some marriages are in shambles today because of an uncontrolled appetite for material things and making more money. Some children are lost to drugs, alcoholism, and gang activities for the same reason. Many of the people of the world know how to take time off to rest and strengthen family ties, but some children of God do not. When their colleagues take time off to rest, the Christian uses that opportunity to acquire more hours (overtime) by covering for them, in order to make more money. When others take time off for birthdays and other holidays, these Christians work the hours for their colleagues' vacations too. This is greed! They think they have good reason to work longer hours than anyone else, but does this really make them happier? No, it does not. They are missing God's best for their lives.

Seek to hear your Father for yourself.

A friend's husband told me that he stopped his job to take care of their children, ages three through eight, because his wife worked two jobs every day, Monday through Friday. She worked every morning and every night on weekdays; that is two full-time jobs. On top of that, she had taken up another weekend job. That means she worked *every day of the week* including weekends. Therefore, this man had decided to quit his job to stay at home and be there for their children each week. Without his wife at home, you can guess where this story is heading. There is no room for God in the whole picture! And yet, they will insist that "God understands." How foolish!

> "For what shall it profit a man, if he shall gains the whole world, and lose his own soul?" *(Mark 8:36)*

You may be laboring in some way, without knowing you are hindering your own growth. The very thing you have been chasing after all these years, and climbing hills and mountains to find, may be right there at your feet. Why don't you know that? Because your spiritual antenna is not in tune with the Lord, you are missing it. Just spend a little while in His presence and stop doing anything that has been keeping you away from your appointments with Jesus, and you can get back to where you ought to be. God does not discourage hard work, by any means, but the truth is that you must get your priorities in order. Esteem His presence first. Do not waste your money on that which is not bread. Do not waste your strength on that which does not profit. Regardless of your career path, you will do a thousand times better if you give more time to personal devotion.

Esteem His presence first.

A key point to assessing the voice of the Lord is meekness. His Word says He will teach the meek in the way (Psalm 25:9). To be meek is to be humble and surrender to His will. God does not speak to everyone.

> And when Saul saw the host of the Philistines, he was afraid, and his heart greatly trembled. And when Saul enquired of the Lord, the Lord answered

him not, neither by dreams, nor by Urim, nor by prophets. *(1 Samuel 28:5-6)*

God only speaks to those who aspire to hear and obey Him. He speaks to those who place value on His Word.

God is speaking to us about abiding in His presence. Reverend Chris Kwakpovwe[3] says, "Avoid the busy lifestyle. It is not how far, but how well (we go) …. Until you learn to discipline, quiet yourself and meditate, or you may not go far in life and ministry." This was the Lord's invitation to Jeremiah the prophet, and I invite you, the reader, to meditate on this message about the Potter and the clay as well.

---

3. Reverend Chris Kwakpovwe, PhD. is the publisher of *Our Daily Manna* devotional.

Chapter Two
WHO IS A POTTER?

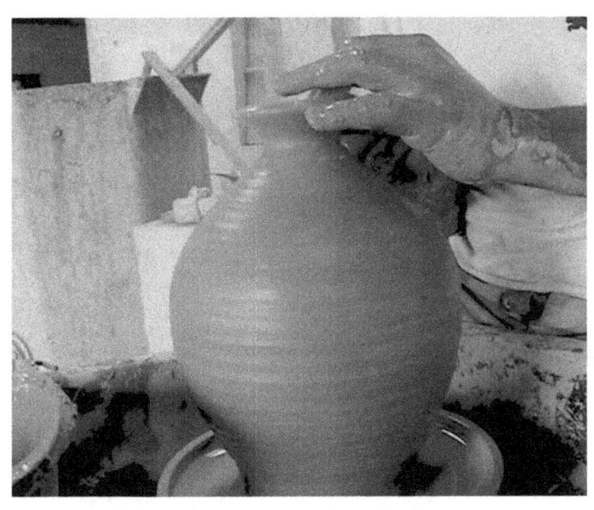

WHO IS A POTTER?

The *Longmans English Larousse* defines a potter as a person who makes pottery. It also defines pottery as clay vessels especially earthenware.[4] In other words, pottery is the potter's craft. It is an art. Jeremiah 18 elaborated further on the role of the potter.

> And the vessel that he made of clay was marred in the hand of the potter; so he made it again into another vessel, as it seemed good to the potter to make." *(Jeremiah 18:4 NKJV)*

The potter is actually an artist. He is creative. He conceives and creates the design of the pot he wants to make depending on its proposed usage. Each design is unique and original. However, in these days of mass production, a potter can decide which design(s) to put in a mold for duplication too. Even so, the initial work is unique. By his design, he transforms the common into something uncommon, the ugly into something beautiful. There are different methods of forming the shape: pinching, coiling, carving, throwing, and casting (mass production). The design, to a large extent, influences his choice of the forming method, but the potter is solely responsible for the design and execution of his work (the pot or vessel).

---

4. Owen C. Watson, *Longman Modern English Dictionary* (Harlow: Longman, 1976).

The Potter

So, who is "the Potter"? The Scripture answers the question in Isaiah 64:

> "Yet you, *Lord*, are our Father. We are the clay, you are *the potter;* we are all the work of your hand."
> *(Isaiah 64:8 NIV, emphasis mine)*

The Lord Almighty is the Master Potter. He is the Potter of potters. In His infinite wisdom, He founded the art of pottery and used it to illustrate His work in the man He created. God is the Potter of all times. He is the Great Artist—the Designer and Creator. He is the Great Craftsman who works in us and with us "to will and to do of his good pleasure" (Philippians 2:13).

Genesis tells how our world was created. It provides the answer to the question man has been researching through philosophy and science. Scripture clearly states that God created the earth and all that is in it including humans who He made in His own image. Genesis 1:26-27 says:

> And God said, Let us make man in our image, after our likeness: and let them have dominion over the fish of the sea, and over the fowl of the air, and over the cattle, and over all the earth, and over every creeping thing that creepeth upon the earth. So God created man in his own image, in the image of God created he him; male and female created he them.
> *(Genesis 1:26-27)*

Here is the comment on this section from the New International Version Life Application Study Bible:

That God created the heavens and the earth is one of the most challenging concepts confronting the modern mind. The vast galaxy we live in is spinning at the incredible speed of 490,000 miles an hour. But even at this breakneck speed, our galaxy still needs 200 million years to make one rotation. And there are over one billion other galaxies just like ours in the universe. Some scientists say that the number of stars in creation is equal to all the grains of all the sands on all the beaches of the world. Yet this complex sea of spinning stars functions with remarkable order and efficiency. To say that the universe "just happened" or "evolved" requires more faith than to believe that God is behind these amazing statistics. God truly did create a wonderful universe.... Almost every ancient religion has its own story to explain how the earth came to be. And almost every scientist has an opinion on the origin of the universe. But only the Bible shows one supreme God creating the earth out of His great love and giving all people a special place in it. We will never know all the answers to how God created the earth, but the Bible tells us that God did create it.[5]

That is the awesome God we serve. He created all things but was not Himself a created being. This book is all about Him and His creative work in man. He is the Potter and He knows the content of each pot (or man) He made. The story of creation teaches us that God is creative. He is eternal and in control of the

---

5. Life Application Study Bible: New International Version. 2017. Carol Stream, IL: Tyndale House Publishers.

world, which includes us, His creation. The earth is the Lord's and the fullness thereof (Psalm 24:1-3).

What Is Clay?

Without bogging you down with too much technical jargon, let's take a look at clay to give us a clearer understanding of the art and the artist. Clay is pliable and responsive earth, which is impressionable when *in a plastic state*. It also refers to decomposed rock which can be made to conform to the potter's form and feeling by the use of water, and then be returned to its rocklike state by being subjected to extreme heat.

Clay is found everywhere. It is one of the most abundant materials on earth. However, clay deposits vary in their chemical composition. This difference is determined by its location, origin, or formation. These factors determine the characteristics or qualities of the clay. This is why a potter finds it easier to work with some particular clays over others. The quality of clay also influences the choice of what the potter plans to make from the clay (the form, size, and function of the vessel).

However, excellent or workable clay may be, it must still undergo a number of purifying processes before it is ready to be used for forming (pot making), display, and even marketing. This is because clay in its natural state looks formless, ugly, and uninteresting. Some bodies of clay are buried deep in the soil. It takes an experienced potter to identify good clay, dig it up, and make it useful and admirable.

A purifying process is also necessary because as clay is transported by agents of erosion, it gets mixed with organic matter, metals, and other impurities. If not properly processed, these materials can pose problems during the shaping process.

Later, when subjected to the usual high heat treatment (or firing) of pots, this organic matter and any volatile oxides burn off, leaving the pot with defects here and there. Therefore, for best results, clay must be thoroughly prepared beforehand. Additionally, no potter wants to work with unprocessed clay because sharp objects might be embedded in it, which could cause serious injury to the potter when he attempts to work with it.

Major Properties of Clay

Plasticity

Clay is *malleable*. It can be pressed or beaten into any shape, without breaking or cracking. For instance, a piece of clay can be rolled into a coil and wound into a loop without breaking. This quality makes it possible for it to be used to make different shapes. In like manner, a Christian should be responsive to the training, shaping, and pruning of the Lord Jesus, his Master.

Workability

This is almost the same thing as plasticity, but it is often influenced by the maturity or aging of the clay. Not all plastic clays are workable. Some are too plastic (fat) and sticky. Workability can be described as the quality of yielding easily to the shaping process.

To the Christian, this is exemplified by the virtue of submission, willing obedience, and readiness for the Master's use.

Porosity

Clay has the ability to absorb water either in its natural state or after bisque firing. Porosity accounts for the way clay pots cool water when used for water storage. The porous pot lets out some water, which the outside air cools, thereby making the pot and the water in it cold. In the spiritual sense, this refers to how we should be open to the Word of God which is scripturally referred to as water, absorbing or assimilating the Word daily, and letting it out again in practical life applications.

Refractoriness

This means clay can withstand very high temperatures. Heat treatment (or firing) is necessary to make the clay vessel permanent and fit for use. Some clay, for example *kaolin*, undergoes temperatures as high as 1400 °C (or 2552 °F) when it is fired. It is in the firing process that the refractory (or heat-resistant) nature of clay is revealed. While high heat is known to destroy most materials, it makes clay stronger and permanent, which is symbolic of toughness. This can be compared to the ability of the believer to withstand hardship. The Bible tells us that we must enter into our inheritance *through many trials.* Jesus suffered to reconcile us to the Father. No servant is greater than his master. Philippians 1 says:

> For it has been granted to you on behalf of Christ
> not only to believe in him, but also to suffer for him.
> *(Philippians 1:29 NIV)*

Again, we are encouraged to endure hardship as good soldiers of the cross. 2 Timothy 2 says:

Thou therefore endure hardness, as a good soldier of
Jesus Christ. *(2 Timothy 2:3)*

Types of Clay

There are two major types of clay: primary and secondary
clay. Primary clay is clay in its original state. It has not been
influenced or contaminated. It is often white or off-white in color.
Secondary clay has been influenced by organic and mineral
impurities. Primary clay can be likened to an inexperienced
Christian. Though a believer, he may not have been exposed
much to those experiences that lead to some godly virtues
like patience, kindness, humility, gentleness, and many others.
Actually, secondary clay is more plastic and workable. Its contact
with other materials through such transportation agents as wind,
flood, stream, other decomposed materials, and its location help
to improve its quality through improved grinding of the particles.
Its color differs according to its experience (secondary location);
it can be pink, brown, ash, dark ash, red, and other colors. Its
exposure or experience makes it richer and a better working
material, just as older Christians should be, especially the ones
that have availed themselves to the Holy Spirit's teaching and
pruning. Nobody truly qualifies to speak about the Master unless
they have a story to tell–stories of persecution, battle, trial, lack,
betrayal, deprivation, pain, divine visitation, victory, and so on.
The Lord uses these experiences to prune us and make us better
working material in his masterful hands.

Pruning is the process of caring for tree branches to make
them more fruitful. Pruned branches are fruitful branches that
have submitted themselves to the direction and correction of the
Lord. They are true followers of Christ who having committed
their lives to Him, and follow Him in obedience daily. In so doing,

they produce much fruit in keeping with their faith. Those who resist the pruning of the Lord are unproductive and as good as dead. The Bible says these will be cut off and tossed aside (John 15:2).

Exposure to the pressures of life help make a man or woman a better material (or clay) in the hand of God; they are more malleable than those that have no stories (or experiences) to tell. The more tests you have been through, the greater your testimony, and the more powerfully you can be used to help others who pass through such situations. As it is written in 2 Corinthians 1:

> Who comforts us in all our troubles, so that we can comfort those in any trouble with the comfort we ourselves receive from God. *(2 Corinthians 1:4 NIV)*

> **Never pray against difficulties or trial, rather ask for the grace to endure and patiently learn the lessons that come with each experience.**

Our experiences spice our lives and make us better tools in God's hands. They may not be palatable, and they may even be painful, but they are necessary to enrich our lives and make us usable by God, the Master Potter. Never pray against difficulties or trial, rather ask for the grace to endure and patiently learn the lessons that come with each experience. Sometimes wonderful gifts are wrapped in unattractive packages. If we base our choices on the way those packages appear, we may unknowingly reject a precious gift.

Sometimes our promotion is preceded by a trial (or trials). These times can threaten us and make us lose focus, sometimes causing us to miss a wonderful opportunity. An example of this is found in the story of Joseph who passed through many trials before he reached the place of his destiny. Even though God had given him dreams revealing that destiny early in life, his life's circumstances seemed to be taking him in an opposite direction. He had to deal with the murderous hatred of his own brothers, being sold into slavery into a foreign land, the pressure of his new master's wife's sexual advances, and finally false sexual harassment allegations which landed him in prison. However, the prison was the narrow road that took him to the palace and brought about the fulfillment of his childhood dream, placing him in the governmental position he was born to fill. When we face unpleasant experiences, we are tempted to doubt God and quit. But if we endure, we will see the hand of the Lord because according to his Word, all things work together for our good.

> And we know that all things work together for good
> to them that love God, to them who are the called
> according to his purpose. *(Romans 8:28)*

Nonplastic clay can hardly be formed into any shape because it is not pliable. It cannot retain shape without support, except by the addition of plastic clay. Any attempt to form it can only succeed as long as the potter is actually holding it. Once he removes his hand, the whole thing crumbles. Nothing can be more frustrating to a potter than working with nonplastic clay. An example of nonplastic clay was Demas, Paul's coworker in 2 Timothy 4:10 who deserted Paul and deserted the faith because he "loved this world." In other words, he loved worldly pleasure more than the call to preach the gospel that God had placed on his life. Demas placed higher value upon what this world has to offer—wealth, power, and pleasure—to the point that he chose to neglect the work God had given him to do. Maybe he was unable to bear the discouragement associated with ministry. Basically, Demas was not yielded to the Holy Spirit. Quitters never win and winners never quit.

Quitters never win and winners never quit.

Child of God, before you quote or sing, "You are the Potter; I am the clay," pause and ask yourself this: *What type of clay am I?* How workable or obedient are you to the Great Potter? Not all clays are workable. How responsive or submissive are you to the masterful hand of the Almighty who desires to shape your life into the vessel He wants you to be? Do you yield easily to Him? Or do you daily frustrate His efforts to shape you? How impressionable are you? Are you alive and responsive to His Word? Does your Christianity end in the church, where you leave the message you heard behind, as you go home and follow your own way? Do you retain what you hear and live it out? *Good clay is impressionable.* It is easy to handle. Its submission culminates in a masterpiece which represents an intimate fusion of the Artist's Spirit with the material He is using.

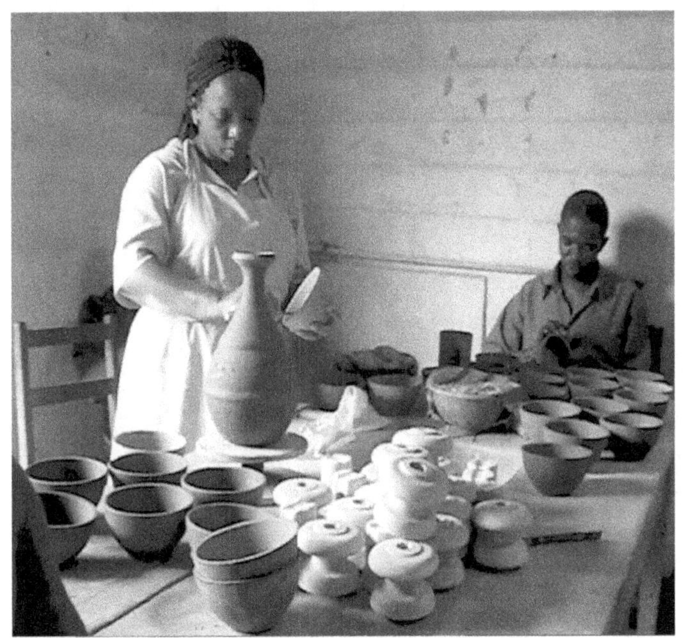

The author working on pottery

Chapter Three
PREPARATION OF THE CLAY

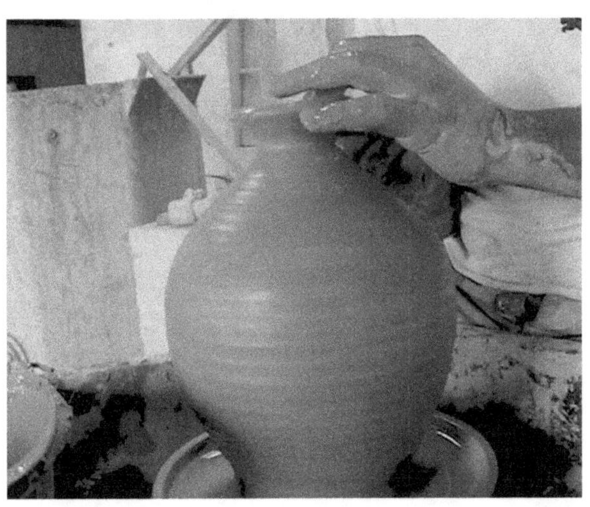

Chapter Three

PREPARATION OF THE CLAY

Once again, we shall take the simplest approach to this process. As soon as clay is sourced or discovered, it is weaned or dug from its deposit. This involves moving it to the place where it will be processed and used.

- **Step 1:** Visible impurities, such as leaves, stones, pebbles, and twigs, are removed by hand.

- **Step 2:** Large lumps of clay are broken down into smaller lumps, using a hammer or wooden crusher.

- **Step 3:** Water is poured into a container and the quantity of clay you desire to process is added. The water should cover the clay and stand at least one inch above it. It is allowed to soak overnight.

- **Step 4:** The soaked clay is thoroughly stirred to obtain a smooth clay slurry.

- **Step 5:** The clay is put through a sieve with a mesh to remove coarse sand and any foreign bodies.

- **Step 6:** The clay is allowed to settle overnight. Then the surplus water is drained off over the sieved clay slip or slurry. (This is the dewatering process).

- **Step 7:** It is stirred very well and poured into a plaster bath to drain off even more water. The Plaster of Paris (or POP) will absorb the excess water, leaving the plastic clay cake ready for use.

51

- **Step 8:** The clay is wrapped and stored in an airtight container to prevent loss of moisture. To age and get the clay more plastic, it is kept in this condition for at least two weeks.

- **Step 9:** The cake is wedged and kneaded the clay. This allows the potter to get the clay to a uniform softness. Water may be added at this stage, if the clay is too hard.

- **Step 10:** The clay is finally ready to use. The potter shapes the clay into his desired form (or pot).

Note that this clay preparation process applies only to the individual/artist potter in a private studio similar to the one Jeremiah visited. In a mass production setting, this process is mostly mechanized.

When the clay has been identified, it is collected and moved to a new environment. First, the clay is moved to the potter's workshop where it will be put to use. For the Christian, when he has given his life to Christ, God leads him to a church or fellowship group where God will be able to work on the young convert, using more experienced Christians to watch over him (discipling), teach him the Scriptures, and impact his life through regular interaction, until he is rooted and built up in Christ.

While doing all this, the young Christian undergoes many changes, including behavioral and association changes. His circle of friends is adjusted. His interests are redirected. His hunger for more of the knowledge of God fuels this. Normally, he desires to fellowship with other believers and pursues spiritual growth while dwelling in God's presence. He no longer enjoys the company of sinners and mockers of God (his old friends). The church or fellowship is the workshop where Christians are purified and groomed by the Lord.

But if we walk in the light as He is in the light, we have fellowship with one another, and the blood of Jesus Christ His Son cleanses us from all sin. *(1 John 1:7 NKJV)*

Today, we hear some people say that you can worship God alone at home. They teach that there is no need for believers to gather together in fellowship. However, the apostles who ran this race before us did get together to worship, study the Word, break bread, and encourage one another. They are our models. Jesus too, walked with others in His ministry. They did not stay alone.

And they continued steadfastly in the apostles' doctrine and fellowship, and in breaking of bread, and in prayers. And fear came upon every soul: and many wonders and signs were done by the apostles. And all that believed were together and had all things in common. *(Acts 2:42-44)*

Not forsaking the assembling of ourselves together, as is the manner of some, but exhorting one another, and so much the more as you see the Day approaching. *(Hebrews 10:25 NKJV)*

The reason for the change in association is clearly stated in these scriptural passages. We fellowship to know Him more, be cleansed, and encourage one another as the Day of the Lord approaches. No Christian can succeed as an island. We need the fellowship of believers. Those who wish to remain alone have often been wounded. Instead of withdrawing, they actually need to form relationships with other Christians, so they can be healed and restored. We need pastors, teachers, and mentors to grow.

On the other hand, the need to break away from old friends and sin partners is emphasized in 2 Corinthians 6:

> Do not be unequally yoked together with unbelievers. For what fellowship has righteousness with lawlessness? And what communion has light with darkness? And what accord has Christ with Belial? Or what part has a believer with an unbeliever? And what agreement has the temple of God with idols? For you are the temple of the living God. As God has said: "I will dwell in them and walk among them. I will be their God, and they shall be My people." Therefore "Come out from among them and be separate, says the Lord. Do not touch what is unclean, and I will receive you." "I will be a Father to you, and you shall be My sons and daughters, says the Lord Almighty." *(2 Corinthians 6:14-18 NKJV)*

Here the Lord emphatically demands that we do this: "Come out from among them and be separate." Again Scripture says:

> Evil communications corrupt good manners. *(1 Corinthians 15:33)*

If we separate ourselves from unbelievers, how will we be able to win them for Christ? An English adage says: "Show me your friend, and I will tell you who you are." Believers are not told to avoid unbelievers; instead they are advised not to form *binding* relationships with them because that will weaken their commitment; and in time, their conduct through compromise with the world. It is difficult to maintain worldly relationships when you do not agree about important life issues, but this does not mean we must sustain total isolation from nonbelieving friends and family. Interestingly Paul also encouraged Christians not to leave their *nonbelieving* spouses! We are encouraged to be active in our witness for Christ to those around us (unbelievers), without entangling ourselves in serious personal, marital, or business commitments with them.

Separation from the world involves more than keeping away from sinful practices; it means maintaining a close relationship with God, first and foremost.

> Blessed is the man who walks not in the counsel of the ungodly, nor stands in the path of sinners, nor sits in the seat of the scornful; but his delight is in the law of the Lord, and in His law he meditates day and night. He shall be like a tree planted by the rivers of water, that brings forth its fruit in its season, whose leaf also shall not wither; and whatever he does shall prosper. *(Psalm 1:1- 3 NKJV)*

The first step in the clay preparation process is spreading it out for drying, and then handpicking impurities, such as leaves and stones. This happens to us when we sit at the Master's feet to hear His voice. He points out those vices in our lives that we need to drop, and the virtues we need to add. It is a part of the cleansing process which the Lord carries out in us as we fellowship with the brethren too.

The next step in the preparation process is that of soaking the clay in water. Water is essential to slake the clay and get it into solution for sieving. Slaking refers to the process in which the clay breaks down into the water. Only when it has broken down in this manner can it be further processed and reused.

Not only is water a natural component of clay, a clay body cannot be plastic or workable without the addition of a *significant volume of water.* This wetting of the clay is a major step in the preparation process. Apart from the removal of impurities, clay preparation is all about wetting the clay until a workable mix is obtained. Initially, excess water is added to slake the clay lumps and form a "sievable" solution. Without water, it will not be easy to get the body into a homogeneous (or uniform) mix. Afterwards, the water is decanted until the sieved clay solidifies into a workable "cake."

To do this, only clean water is can be used. Water is vital for the survival of man and all living things, and drinking impure water can lead to serious health hazards, even death. Similarly, the use of water contaminated by any type of oil or soap will result in contamination of the clay. These cannot give a successful end result.

As water is to the clay, so is the Word of God to us as Christians.

Spiritually speaking, water is symbolic of the Word of God, and the Word of God is necessary for salvation as well as for shaping the Christian into the vessel God wants him to be. The Scripture says:

> So then faith comes by hearing, and hearing by the word of God. *(Romans 10:17 NKJV)*

> That He might sanctify and cleanse her with the washing of *water* by the word *(Ephesians 5:26 NKJV)*

> To those who were disobedient long ago when God waited patiently in the days of Noah while the ark was being built. In it only a few people, eight

in all, were saved through *water*, and this *water* symbolizes baptism that now saves you also–not the removal of dirt from the body but the pledge of a clear conscience toward God. It saves you by the resurrection of Jesus Christ" (1 Peter 3:20–21 NIV)

Again, the one who delights in meditating on the Word of God is likened to a tree planted by the streams of water, which yields its fruit in season, as quoted earlier. From this, we can see that water (the Word of God) is necessary for our growth and fruitfulness.

You are already clean because of the word I have spoken to you…If you remain in me and my words remain in you, ask whatever you wish, and it will be done for you. This is my Father's glory, that *you bear much fruit*, showing yourselves to be my disciples. *(John 15:3, 7-8 NIV)*

As water is to the clay, so is the Word of God to us as Christians. God reveals Himself to us through His Word. As water makes clay workable, so does the Word of God sustain us, helping us to grow, and be fruitful. The Word of God is the spiritual life and energy of every Christian.

Everything came into existence through the Word of God, and it is the only thing that can sustain us in our walk with the Lord. We need it to maintain God's standard, the lifestyle of His kingdom. We need the Word for a healthy spiritual diet to maintain our stability. His Word is Spirit. The Word of God is what we need for salvation, healing, deliverance, revival, restoration, prayer, and so much more.

When we have the Word in the right proportion in our lives, every other thing falls into place, just as it does for the clay, which requires just the right amount of water to become plastic in the hands of the potter. *And it is a lot of water, not a little!* Even in prayer, the Word of God is important. We cannot maintain a fervent prayer life without the Word. Without it we cannot argue any case either. The Lord says, "Come now let us reason together" (Isaiah 1:18). How can we reason with God if we cannot present His Word to Him? That is the method we are supposed to use to remind Him of His promises! The wisdom we need to preserve our lives and prosper is also tied to God's Word.

> How can a young man cleanse his way? By taking heed according to Your word. With my whole heart I have sought You; oh, let me not wander from Your commandments! Your word I have hidden in my heart, that I might not sin against You. *(Psalm 119:9–11 NKJV)*

Another vital stage in clay preparation is *the waiting period.* It is the time when the clay is wrapped up and allowed to age. Freshly prepared clay is usually not very workable. For this reason, an experienced potter knows he needs to cover up the clay and wait for some time before putting it to use. This makes his job easier because the clay's enhanced plasticity enables him to manipulate the clay more efficiently for the best result.

Waiting can be seen in tree growth too. The tree that grows tall doesn't necessarily grow very fast initially, like grasses do. A tree takes time to develop its roots downwards. Outwardly, it may seem as if it is not growing at all, but it is preparing for its massive trunk by developing the roots that will carry that weight.

God can use a young convert, but there is a limit to what he can be used for until he matures. A young Christian is a spiritual baby; therefore, he can only talk, move, and act like a baby. This maturation process is when a Christian is groomed and prepared for divine service by the interplay of the Holy Spirit, the Word, and discipleship or mentoring. It is a period of inward growth, when the child of God puts down deep roots in Christ.

> As newborn babes, desire the pure milk of the word, that you may grow thereby. *(1 Peter 2:2 NKJV)*

> And being assembled together with them, He commanded them not to depart from Jerusalem, but to wait for the Promise of the Father, "which," He said, "you have heard from Me; for John truly baptized with water, but you shall be baptized with the Holy Spirit not many days from now." *(Acts 1:4-5 NKJV)*

This spiritual aging process (maturity) is not tied to any specified time period. It varies from individual to individual, but it is dependent on the person's willingness to learn and grow—their spiritual hunger. It also depends on the believer's availability to the grooming of the Holy Spirit, the Word, and other agencies. Look again at Acts 1:4-5 above. This is the direction the apostles were given. They waited in prayer, studying God's Word, and then came the empowerment of the Holy Spirit, which can be described as their commissioning for ministry.

After the aging process comes the wedging and kneading of the clay. This involves the use of pressure to force out air pockets and homogenize the body to soften any hidden lumps. Wedging is necessary to bring the clay to a uniform smoothness.

More water can be added if required. It further enhances the plasticity and workability of the clay.

This can be likened to the experiences a Christian undergoes that better prepares him to be used by God. Some of these experiences may not be pleasant, especially when pressure, persecution, pain, trials, temptations, want, and suffering are involved. The apostle Paul in narrating his own experience said this in 2 Corinthians 11:

> From the Jews five times I received forty stripes minus one. Three times I was beaten with rods; once I was stoned…in weariness and toil, in sleeplessness often, in hunger and thirst, in fastings often, in cold and nakedness–besides the other things; what comes upon me daily: my deep concern for all the churches. Who is weak, and I am not weak? Who is made to stumble, and I do not burn with indignation? *(2 Corinthians 11:24-25, 27-29 NKJV)*

He also said this:

> Who shall separate us from the love of Christ? Shall tribulation, or distress, or persecution, or famine, or nakedness, or peril, or sword?...Yet in all these things we are more than conquerors through Him who loved us. For I am persuaded that neither death nor life, nor angels nor principalities…nor any other created thing, shall be able to separate us from the love of God which is in Christ Jesus our Lord. *(Romans 8:35, 37-39 NKJV)*

We should therefore face any unpleasant situation in this race with the same resolve, holding onto the fact that nothing can separate us from the love of God. All our experiences are actually working together for our good, even though we may not understand that now. Job said he would come forth as gold after he had been tested (Job 23:10). And so shall we in Jesus' name!

> **All our experiences are actually working together for our good, even though we may not understand that now.**

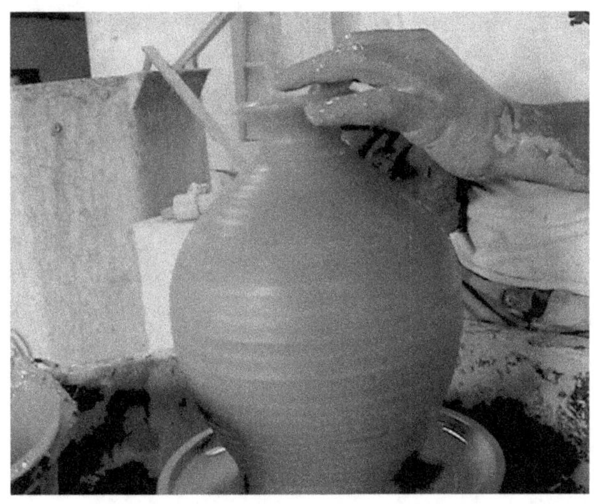

Forming a pottery vase from clay

SIZE, DESIGN AND FUNCTION

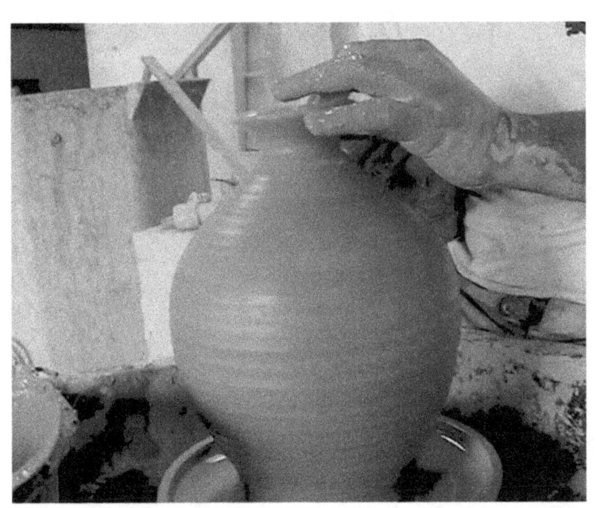

Chapter Four

SIZE, DESIGN AND FUNCTION

Pottery sizes and designs are most often influenced by the intended use of the vessel. For instance, large clay wine or water pots, which are not meant to be lifted most of the time, are designed with short necks and wide rims with the intent that smaller containers (cups or mugs) will be able to pass through them to draw out the wine or water, whatever the case may be. We see this in John 2:

> Jesus told the servants, "Fill the jars with water." When the jars had been filled, he said, "Now dip some out, and take it to the master of ceremonies." So the servants followed his instructions. *(John 2:7-8 NLT)*

Such large pots may not require handles since they are not meant to be lifted frequently. Where handles are attached at all, they are often "false handles" and only intended to be decorative.

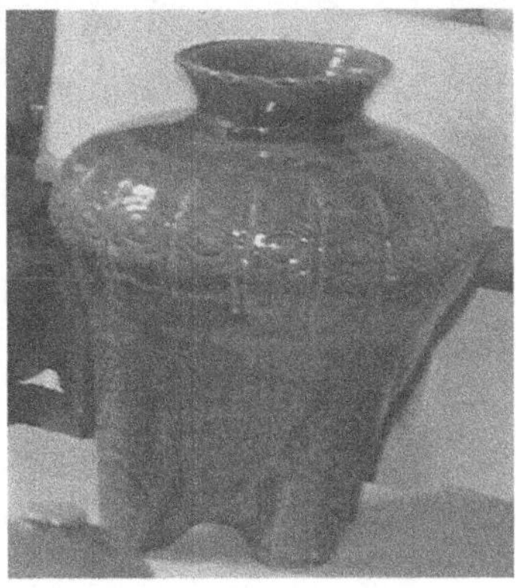

Four-Footed Pot by the author

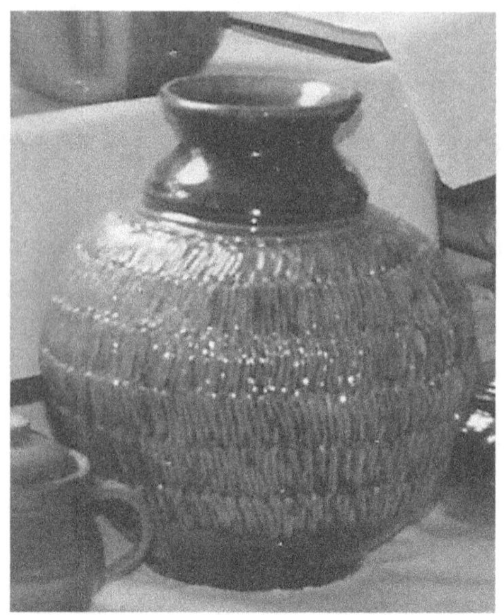

Relief Decorated Pot by the author

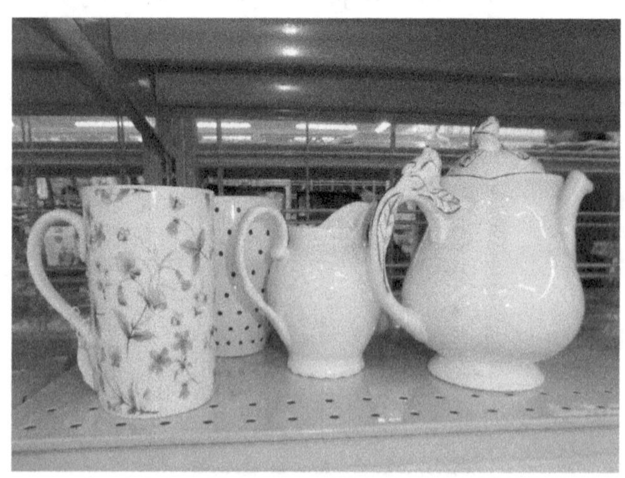

Tea Pottery

Vessels for drinking, such as pitchers, mugs, coffee, and tea cups are designed to be easily carried with one hand. They are made small in size. They also require handles for convenience. They are designed to have narrow rims and made as light as possible for easy handling. Plates and bowls for eating are designed with wide rims, and are flat or low in height. This is to allow the user to see the inside clearly so they can handle the contents.

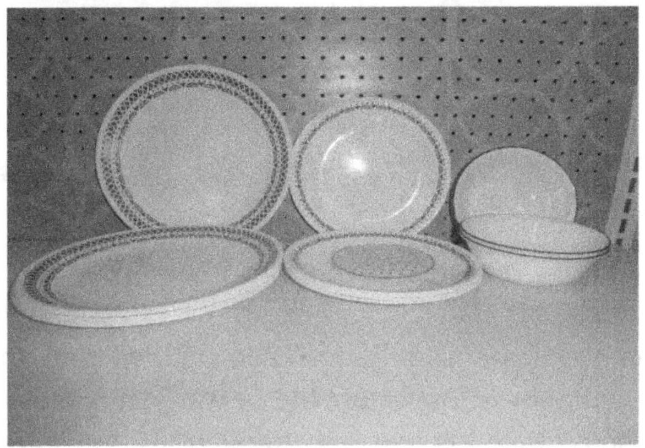

Pottery Dinner wares

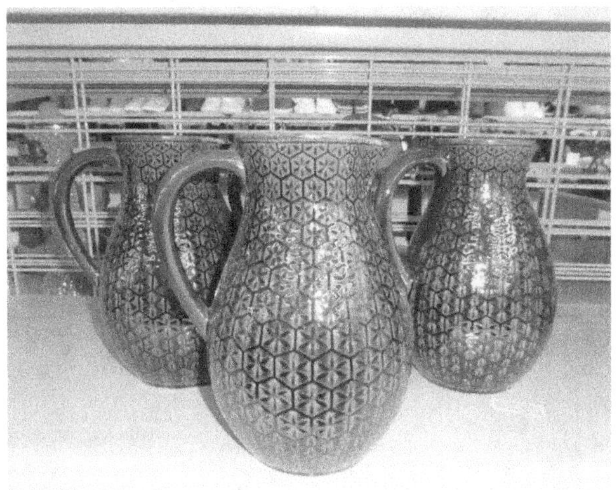

Pottery Water Pitchers

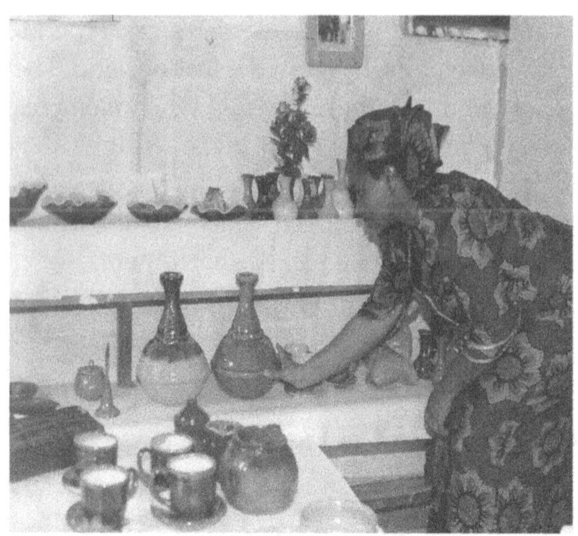

Assorted Pottery wares by the author

Flower vases are usually designed with elegant and narrow necks to enable them to protect the flower stems they will hold, keeping them close together as arranged. The designs are also made as simple as possible to avoid taking away from the beauty of the flowers themselves. The flowers are meant to be the center of attention, not the vase.

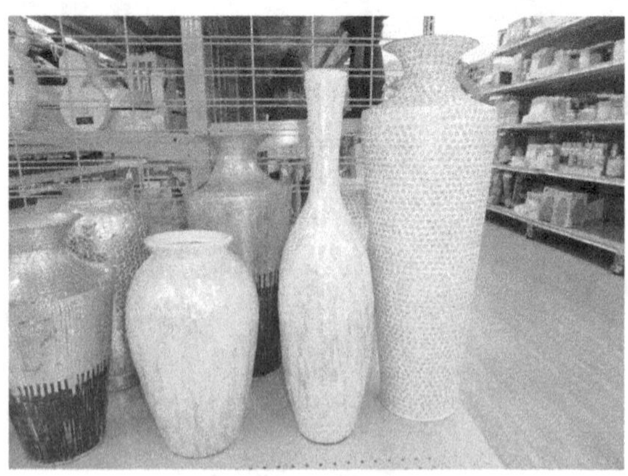

Decorative Pots

Water and wine pitchers are designed to be moderately sized for easy hand lifting. Their necks are also made just wide enough to provide an easy flow of their contents. For this reason, pitchers must have handles and good spouts too.

This is why God designs each of us differently too. What He makes of any individual depends on His intended purpose for that person. There is, therefore, no need for anybody to force himself to be like someone else, and there is also no need to force another person to be like you. This is why there are extroverts and introverts. Every one of us was created with a different personality and fitted to a specific task. Our temperaments are also different and unique, so some people thrive better than others under certain circumstances. Some people are good leaders, and others are better followers. While some people are inspirational speakers, others are good listeners. God made us all; we are His and He made us for His pleasure. If God made you a good follower, there is no need to force yourself into being a leader or vice versa. What one naturally enjoys doing what one does effortlessly, this is an indication of God's calling. For instance, when you give the microphone to someone who is gifted in teaching, he or she can talk for hours without running out of words or inspiration. Someone who is not a teacher will find it very difficult to speak for even a few minutes before he or she gives up for lack of material. They have not been formed by the Master Potter for that task. Each of us should find ways of developing ourselves along the lines of those things we enjoy doing which are not sinful. In so doing, we will find God's best for our lives. These areas must be the potential that can be harnessed for the service of God and humanity. If you enjoy writing, acting, praying, serving others, teaching, whatever it is, use it for the service of God and your fellow men.

For just as each of us has one body with many members, and these members do not all have the same function, so in Christ we, though many, form one body, and each member belongs to all the others. We have different gifts, according to the grace given to each of us. If your gift is prophesying, then prophesy in accordance with your faith; if it is serving, then serve; if it is teaching, then teach; if it is to encourage, then give encouragement; if it is giving, then give generously; if it is to lead, do it diligently; if it is to show mercy, do it cheerfully. *(Romans 12:4-8 NIV)*

The Master Potter who made us knows why He made us.

The Master Potter who made us knows why He made us. He has placed within us the necessary ingredients required to fulfill those purposes. This is why people behave, most often, the way they are designed to behave, and not the way we expect them to behave. Therefore, it should not bother us when those around us—at home, church, or our workplace behave differently than we do. We should expect that! We can accommodate them and encourage them to discover God's purpose for their lives, instead of making fruitless efforts to change them.

Any married couple who does not understand this undergoes massive friction in their relationship. Many marriages are on the rocks for this reason. Opposites attract, and they are meant to make up for what is lacking in each other; they should not focus on one another's weaknesses. A man's area of weakness might be his wife's area of strength and vice versa. When the two come together with the right attitude, accepting each other with love, and focusing on the positive, they are both strengthened.

We have not been called to change people. Doing this is a frustrating proposition. We are mandated to preach the gospel of salvation to the perishing. It is God's sole responsibility to transform them into the vessels He wants them to be. Among genuine believers, we are not bound to behave alike. The same God works in us all to do and to will of His good pleasure (Philippians 2:13).

> ## We have not been called to change people.

Uses of Pottery

Pottery is used for various purposes—domestic, social, aesthetic and religious uses. Pottery making is practiced by many as a career and a money-making venture.

Domestic Uses

Pottery is used in homes and the hospitality industry for serving food and drinks. In our homes and in restaurants, we use dinner sets, tea sets, water and wine pitchers (jugs), mugs, and various storage vessels. In Genesis 24:15, we read about Rebekah fetching water with a water jar (very likely a clay pot) on her shoulder when Abraham's chief servant was looking for a wife for Isaac. The servant met her there, and was impressed with her. This is an indication that clay pots were commonly used in biblical times.

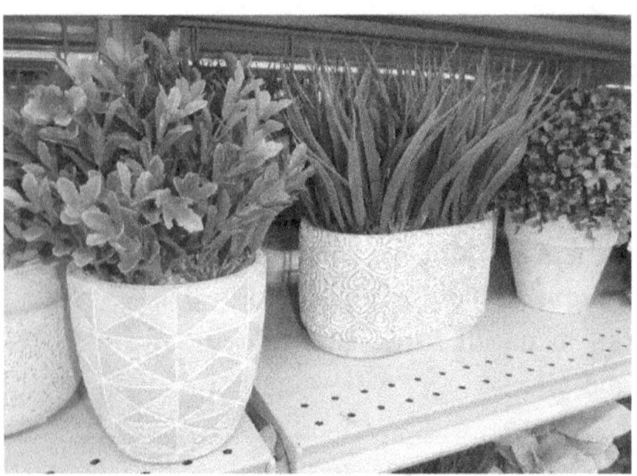

Pottery Planters

Social Uses

Among the Igbo people of Nigeria, large clay pots are used to store palm wine during ceremonies, especially traditional marriage. The pots serve as standard palm wine measurement on ceremonial occasions. At a wedding in Cana of Galilee, Jesus turned water into wine. Before this happened, Jesus instructed them to do this:

> Jesus saith unto them, Fill the waterpots with water.
> And they filled them up to the brim. *(John 2:7)*

These were likely clay pots. This shows that clay pots played an important role in Jewish social life.

Aesthetics

Pottery can be designed for aesthetic or decorative purposes— indoors and out. These are called ornamental or decorative wares. Among them are flower vases and planters, figurines, wall hangings, and all sorts of beautiful objects. These items are made for the beautification of homes, hotels, and public buildings. They showcase the competence of the potter (artist), and are pleasurable to behold. Because they beautify the environment, they promote a sense of peace and mental and psychological relaxation in the space in which they stand. In some cases, people use them as means of displaying their affluence. Poor people can hardly be art collectors because art works are usually expensive.

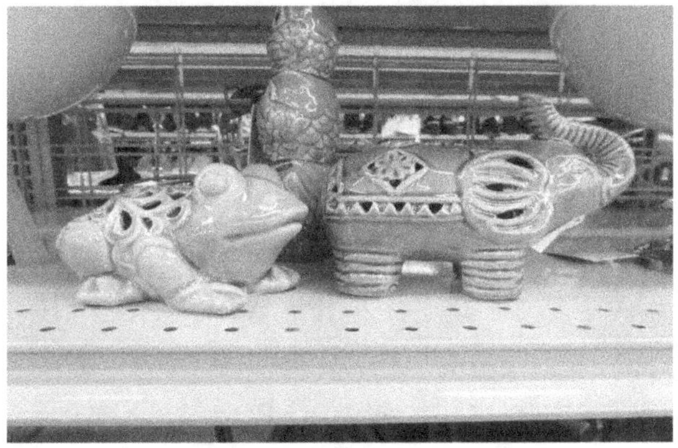

Decorative Sculptural Pottery

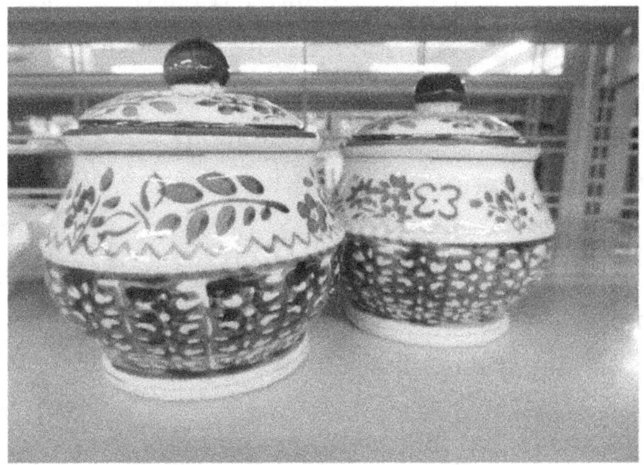

Decorated Sugar Bowls

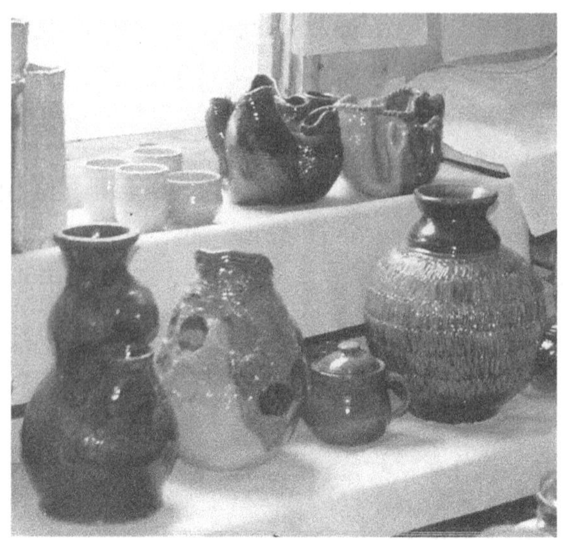

Assorted Pottery by the author

We are His creative work, and He admires all our differences in size, height, shape, and complexion.

Just as the potter will create a figurine because he finds it beautiful, God created us for His pleasure. We are His creative work, and He admires all our differences in size, height, shape, and complexion. He actually made us each intentionally unique! If we understand this, we will reject the concept of an inferiority complex. We should accept ourselves the way we are made. If anybody has any complaint with respect to their physique, he may petition our Creator as he likes, but the Lord is sovereign. There is no justification for self-hatred or complaints about our natural appearance.

God saw all that he had made, and it was very good. *(Genesis 1:31 NIV)*

Religious Uses

Some people use pottery as objects of idol worship. They actually believe there are gods who are in control of the pottery craft and that nobody gets involved in the business of pottery making until he or she receives permission from those gods. In other places, anybody can engage in pot making, but ritual pots are said to be made by special potters appointed by the god(s). These potters are usually the priestesses of the clay god or goddess. These practices still go on today in some countries, but is based on witchcraft and superstition, neither of which is the focus of this book.

Churches and fellowship groups commonly use pottery too. They may use a chalice, ciborium (a covered metal vessel), and saucers as utilitarian objects for serving the elements in Holy Communion. They are also used as candle stands and flower vases for decoration.

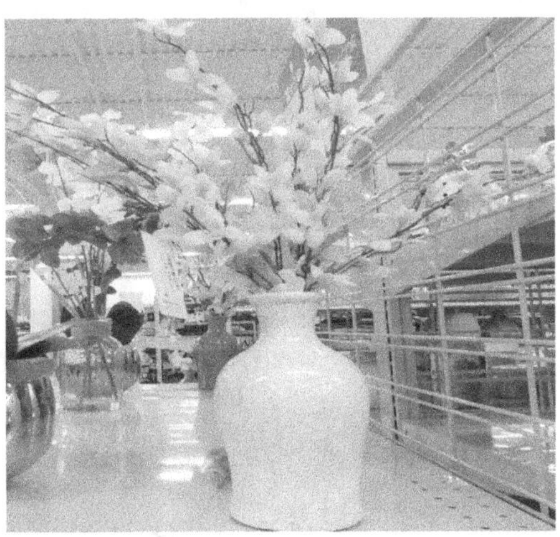

Pottery Flower vase

Livelihood

Pottery is a viable means of making money to support yourself. As a career, a potter can be gainfully employed in the ceramic industry, work for himself in a private studio, and engage in consultancy services. Business people engage in pottery collecting for money-making ventures. A potter's products are in high demand because of their wide usage. Professional potters also work as instructors and lecturers in schools, colleges, universities, and research institutes.

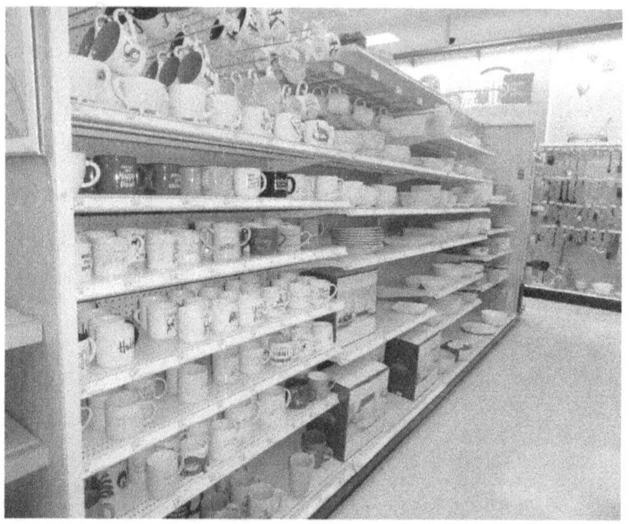

Commercial Pottery

The Scriptural Symbolism of Pottery

Common

The precious sons of Zion, valuable as fine gold, how they are regarded as clay pots, the work of the hands of the potter! *(Lamentations 4:2 NKJV)*

The sons of Zion were once considered as valuable and highly priced as gold, but they lost their value and became as common and cheap as pottery. Clay wares or pottery are represented as affordable and readily available (common). This is possibly due to the abundance of the raw material. Clay is virtually found everywhere. However, the quality differs from place to place.

Weakness

> Whereas you saw the feet and toes, partly of potter's clay and partly of iron, the kingdom shall be divided; yet the strength of the iron shall be in it, just as you saw the iron mixed with ceramic clay. And as the toes of the feet were partly of iron and partly of clay, so the kingdom shall be partly strong and partly fragile. *(Daniel 2:41-42 NKJV)*

In this passage, the potter's clay, a fragile or weak mineral, represents the weak nature of a coming kingdom, while iron represents the strength of the coming kingdom with which it will break in pieces and crush all the other kingdoms.

> To this very day, God still looks for available men and women into which He will pour His own wisdom, strength, and power to fulfill His divine purposes.

The Lord carefully chose to use clay, an earthy material, out of all the numerous minerals He created to illustrate His work in mankind. When He chose us, He was not looking for very strong or wise men. He was looking for available materials. To this very day, God still looks for available men and women into which He will pour His own wisdom, strength, and power to fulfill His divine purposes. Therefore, we do not need to possess special abilities to be used of God.

> For you see your calling, brethren, that not many wise according to the flesh, not many mighty, not many noble, are called. But God has chosen the foolish things of the world to put to shame the wise, and God has chosen the weak things of the world to put to shame the things which are mighty. *(1 Corinthians 1:26-27 NKJV)*

Ordinary (or Unadorned)

> If you only look at us, you might well miss the brightness. We carry this precious Message around in the unadorned clay pots of our ordinary lives. That's to prevent anyone from confusing God's incomparable power with us. *(2 Corinthians 4:7 MSG)*

New International Version Life Application Bible comments on this passage as follows:

> "The supremely valuable message of salvation in Jesus Christ has been entrusted by God to frail and fallible human beings ("jars of clay"). Paul's focus, however, was not on the perishable container but on its content–God's power dwelling in us. Though we are weak, God uses us to spread his Good News, and he gives us power to do his work. Knowing that

the power is his, not ours, should keep us from pride and motivate us to keep daily contact with God, our power source. Our responsibility is to let people see God through us."[6]

This scriptural passage portrays vessels of clay (or pottery) as unadorned, ordinary, not special but common, objects. Here, ordinary men (mere humans), easily available men, are described as clay pots, used by God to do extraordinary things. He does this, so that the glory for his exploits may be His alone. God does not want anyone to take the glory for what He uses that person to do. He told Gideon that the men he brought out for the battle against the Midianites were *too many*, lest Israel take the glory for their victory, thinking that their own hands had wrought it. God wants us to be exactly what He made us to be; He simply wants to partner with us and guide us throughout our lives.

Many people misunderstand 2 Timothy 2:20, thinking it means that clay vessels represent instruments for dishonorable use. This passage outlines different categories of vessels in a kitchen, among them earthenware (or clay or ceramic vessels). After the categorization, it goes on to classify the uses of those kitchen items—some to honor and some to dishonor.

> Now in a large house there are not only gold and silver vessels, but also vessels of wood and of earthenware, and some to honor and some to dishonor. *(2 Timothy 2:20 NASB)*

> In a well-furnished kitchen there are not only crystal goblets and silver platters, but waste cans

6. Life Application Study Bible: New International Version. 2017. Carol Stream, IL: Tyndale House Publishers.

and compost buckets–some containers used to serve fine meals, others to take out the garbage. *(2 Timothy 2:20 MSG)*

What this passage is really saying is that a well-furnished kitchen contains an assortment of beautiful serving dishes and plates, amongst them ceramic plates (pottery or earthenware). Virtually all modern kitchens and restaurants use beautiful ceramic plates to serve their meals. Is this an ignoble or dishonorable use? No! Ceramics are actually the most popular among the vessels mentioned. They are among the ones used to "honor" or "serve fine meals." However, there are other vessels in the kitchen that you must wash your hands after touching, such as garbage cans and compost buckets.

God still retains the power to decide to make vessels for noble (honorable) or common (ignoble) use, but not all clay vessels are designated common or ignoble by the Scriptures.

But who are you, a human being, to talk back to God? "Shall what is formed say to the one who formed it, 'Why did you make me like this?'" Does not the potter have the right to make out of the same lump of clay some pottery for noble purposes and some for common use? *(Romans 9:20-21 NIV)*

The Message translation states it this way:

Who in the world do you think you are to second-guess God? Do you for one moment suppose any of us knows enough to call God into question? Clay doesn't talk back to the fingers that mold it, saying, "Why did you shape me like this?" Isn't it obvious that a potter has a perfect right to shape one lump of clay into a vase for holding flowers and another into a pot for cooking beans? If God needs one style of pottery especially designed to show his angry displeasure and another style carefully crafted to show his glorious goodness, isn't that all right? Either or both happens to Jews, but it also happens to the other people. *(Romans 9:20-24 MSG)*

Chapter Five

GOD: THE MASTER POTTER

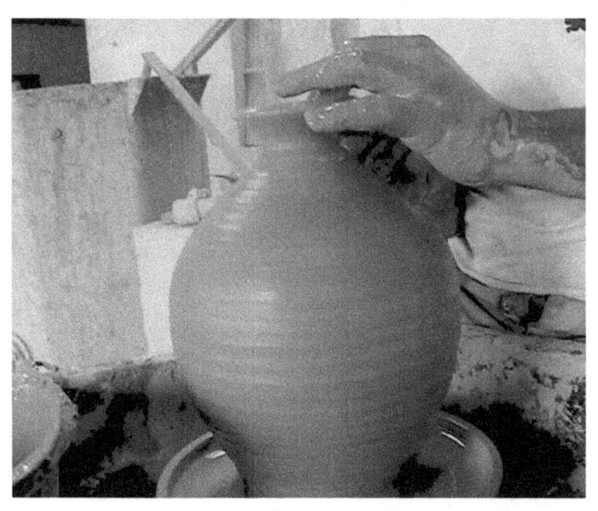

GOD: THE MASTER POTTER

**"O house of Israel, can I not do with you
as this potter has done?" says the Lord.
"Behold, like the clay in the potter's hand, so
are you in my hand, O house of Israel."
—Jeremiah 18:6 RSV**

Yet you, Lord, are our Father. We are the clay, you
are the potter; we are all the work of your hand.
(Isaiah 64:8 NIV)

Like clay in the hand of a potter, so are you in the hand
of your Maker, oh, child of God! If that is true (and it
is), then you are only a raw material in the hand of a
manufacturer. It takes a potter to identify and make something
worthwhile from clay. Only the potter can identify the potential
in the clay, and take the necessary steps to maximize its usage.
Without the potter, nobody would ever hear about clay or think
of putting it to use. No wonder the Lord said this concerning
Jeremiah:

"Before I formed you in the womb I knew you, before
you were born I set you apart." *(Jeremiah 1:5 NIV)*

If the clay makes any contribution to its end use, it is that
of submissiveness—submitting to the masterful hands of the

potter. This alone is what is required of the clay. The clay does not determine what it is used for or how. It is completely up to the potter to employ his skill and decide the best use for any clay.

> Does not the potter have the right to make out of the same lump of clay some pottery for special purposes and some for common use? *(Romans 9:21 NIV)*

If the clay makes any contribution to its end use, it is that of submissiveness

---

As a mere medium or instrument, the clay is expected to yield itself to be used of the potter, and not vice versa. The Scripture says:

> You turn things upside down, as if the potter were thought to be like the clay! Shall what is formed say to the one who formed it, "You did not make me"? Can the pot say to the potter, "You know nothing"? *(Isaiah 29:16 NIV)*

Asking the questions found above amounts to rebellion and stubbornness. A child of God that acts in this way, stands the risk of being abandoned for more submissive materials. No potter would like to use nonplastic clay because it cannot be easily manipulated or shaped. This is why plasticity is one of the primary qualities of good clay, especially if it will be used for pot making. Any vessel God will use to accomplish His purpose must be totally and unconditionally submissive.

> Any vessel God will use to accomplish His purpose must be totally and unconditionally submissive.

In Judges 4, the Lord commanded Barak, son of Abinoam, through Deborah to take with him ten thousand men to go and fight against Jabin, a king of Canaan, who reigned in Hazor.

She (Deborah) sent for Barak son of Abinoam from Kedesh in Naphtali and said to him, "The Lord, the God of Israel, commands you: 'Go, take with you ten thousand men of Naphtali and Zebulun and lead them up to Mount Tabor. I will lead Sisera, the commander of Jabin's army, with his chariots and his troops to the Kishon River and give him into your hands.'" Barak said to her, "If you go with me, I will go; but if you don't go with me, I won't go." "Certainly I will go with you," said Deborah. "But because of the course you are taking, the honor will not be yours, for the Lord will deliver Sisera into the hands of a woman." So Deborah went with Barak to Kedesh. There Barak summoned Zebulun and Naphtali, and ten thousand men went up under his command. Deborah also went up with him. *(Judges 4:6-10 NIV, addition mine)*

Take note that Barak told Deborah this:

"If you go with me, I will go; but if you don't go with me, I won't go." *(Judges 4:8 NIV)*

This is a clear case of *conditional* obedience or submission. Barak was either cowardly or in need of human support. Either way, he didn't step out according to the prophetic command, as someone who trusted God. Deborah told him that God would be with him in the battle, but even with that reassurance, he was still not courageous. His request that Deborah should go with him showed that he trusted human strength more than God's promise. Real faith would have stepped out, trusting that He who promised was able to see him through. Barak didn't have to depend on human support.

Nevertheless, because Deborah was zealous for God and courageous, she accepted the situation and went with them into battle. However, the glory of the victory in that battle went to a woman—Jael, the wife of Heber the Kenite, just as Deborah had prophesied. Jael was the one the Lord eventually used to kill Sisera, the commander of Jabin's army (Judges 4:16-22). This showed God's disapproval of Barak's conditional obedience to His call.

In 1 Kings 17, we read the story of the widow at Zarephath:

Some time later the brook dried up because there had been no rain in the land. Then the word of the Lord came to him: "Go at once to Zarephath in the region of Sidon and stay there. I have directed a widow there to supply you with food." So he went to Zarephath. When he came to the town gate, a widow was there gathering sticks. He called to her and asked, "Would you bring me a little water in a jar so I may have a drink?" As she was going to get it, he called, "And bring me, please, a piece of bread." "As surely as the Lord your God lives," she replied, "I don't have any bread–only a handful of flour in a jar and a little olive oil in a jug. I am gathering a few sticks to take home and make a meal for myself and my son, that we may eat it–and die." Elijah said to her, "Don't be afraid. Go home and do as you have said. But first make a small loaf of bread for me from what you have and bring it to me, and then make something for yourself and your son. For this is what the Lord, the God of Israel, says: 'The jar of flour will not be used up and the jug of oil will not run dry until the day the Lord sends rain on the land.'" She went away and did as Elijah had told her. So there was food every day for Elijah and for the woman and her family. For the jar of flour was not used up and the jug of oil did not run dry, in keeping with the word of the Lord spoken by Elijah. *(1 Kings 17:7-16 NIV)*

The famine in the land was so severe because it had not rained for a few years. Not only was the widow's food almost completely exhausted, but she didn't have any hope of getting any more food anywhere else. There was nowhere to buy food, even if she had money. That meant she had no hope of accessing food for her family. She was in a humanly hopeless situation at the time, but this widow was a wonderful example in submission: she was very plastic clay indeed.

That day, she went out to the city gate to gather firewood to cook what she thought would be their last meal. Elijah interrupted her by asking her to go and get him some water to drink. She obliged him. As if that was not enough, he also requested a piece of bread as she stepped out to get the water. In our world of abundance, it is hard to imagine what it was like for this woman and her son; but at this time, a piece of bread was no small thing. A piece of bread represented an entire meal—for a whole family. The widow protested but did not disobey.

She told Elijah her situation, but still did as he bid her. Her situation was this: She only had a handful of flour and a little oil to make a cake for her and her son. Her plan was that they would eat one last meal together before they died. On top of the fact that Elijah asked for food and water, he also asked her to prepare *his food first*. That meant there was no guarantee that she and her son would eat anything! Even so, this widow obeyed and submitted to the servant of God, as unto the Lord. She submitted without counting the cost. She obeyed without trying to negotiate her reward.

She obeyed without trying to negotiate her reward.

God might be making a demand on an area of your need too. This might be an area in which you are still crying for His help or intervention, but God's plan is to bless you more than you can imagine. He never makes a demand on any area of our lives in which He has not planned to visit us.

Just as clay does not negotiate with the Potter before it submits to His touch, we can never choose to obey for what we will receive. Trying to negotiate with God before submission can make you lose His blessing. He has better plans for you than you can imagine.

> For as high as the heavens are above the earth, so great
> is his love for those who fear him. *(Psalm 103:11 NIV)*

In Luke 5, when Jesus told Peter to "launch out into the deep," it was not just for a large catch of fish. Though the immediate result was a large catch of fish, Jesus had much more in mind than that for Peter. The greater result the great pile of fish had was to take Peter to another level spiritually. The purpose of the revelation Peter had was to make him a fisher of men—bringing him into God's ultimate will for his life. When you obey God, leave everything to Him because He will accomplish much more than you are able to ask or imagine. Note that in Luke 5:5, human reasoning nearly robbed Peter of his wonderful blessing. Peter said:

> "Master, we've worked hard all night and haven't caught anything. But because you say so, I will let down the nets." *(Luke 5:5 NIV)*

When you obey God, leave everything to Him because He will accomplish much more than you are able to ask or imagine.

Physically speaking, Peter was an experienced fisherman, and nobody would have blamed him for his comment or opinion, but the issue remains that obedience to God is a work of faith. God's plan might not mesh well with human reasoning or professional skill.

> The mind governed by the flesh (sinful mind) is hostile to God; it does not submit to God's law, nor can it do so. Those who are in the realm of

the flesh (controlled by it) cannot please God. *(Romans 8:7-8 NIV, additions mine)*

God's plan might not mesh well with human reasoning or professional skill.

Many Christians have lost their divine visitation due to carnal reasoning, leading to disobedience. Knowledge is important just like obedience, but knowledge becomes dangerous when it challenges the ability of God. When we allow our thoughts to convince us to not submit to God, or lead us to doubt His power, we can miss His plan for our life. Thank God for Peter who did not give in to this temptation. Instead Peter listened to Jesus and let down his nets again. Peter said:

"Nevertheless at thy word I will let down the net."
(Luke 5:5b)

In other words, Peter was saying my professional skill tells me I can't catch any fish right now, but because You can do all things, I will obey You, and do what You say, even though it doesn't make any natural sense to me at all. Obedience to God is wholly a walk of faith. Look at the result:

When they had done so, they caught such a large number of fish that their nets began to break. So they signaled their partners in the other boat to come and help them, and they came and filled their boats so full that they began to sink. *(Luke 5:6-7 NIV)*

This was a miracle, wasn't it? Perhaps if they had brought four or more boats, they would have been filled with fish as well. Another example of this kind of situation in the Word can be found in the case of the dead prophet's wife in 2 Kings 4:

> The wife of a man from the company of the prophets cried out to Elisha, "Your servant my husband is dead, and you know that he revered the Lord. But now his creditor is coming to take my two boys as his slaves." Elisha replied to her, "How can I help you? Tell me, what do you have in your house?" "Your servant has nothing there at all," she said, "except a small jar of olive oil." Elisha said, "Go around and ask all your neighbors for empty jars. Don't ask for just a few. Then go inside and shut the door behind you and your sons. Pour oil into all the jars, and as each is filled, put it to one side." She left him and shut the door behind her and her sons. They brought the jars to her and she kept pouring. When all the jars were full, she said to her son, "Bring me another one." But he replied, "There is not a jar left." Then the oil stopped flowing. She went and told the man of God, and he said, "Go, sell the oil and pay your debts. You and your sons can live on what is left." *(2 Kings 4:1-7 NIV).*

God will always honor obedience.

This woman was facing a terrible crisis. Not only was she in pain and grieved because of the loss of her husband, she was also at the point of losing her two sons due to inherited debt! However, she was a woman of faith. She trusted God and believed His prophet. What happened? All her problems were solved in a moment in a miraculous way because of a simple act of obedience. God will always honor obedience. All the containers she had and those she borrowed were filled before the flow of oil ceased, so when the Lord tells you to gather vessels or containers, gather as many as possible. Elisha had told her to bring your vessels "not a few" (2 Kings 4:3 KJV).

> Hear me, O Judah, and ye inhabitants of Jerusalem; believe in the Lord your God, so shall ye be established; believe his prophets, so shall ye prosper. *(2 Chronicles 20:20b)*

As you yield yourself totally to the Master Potter, you will have nothing to regret.

In each of these cases, God proved Himself to be the Almighty. The results were professionally inexplicable. As you yield yourself totally to the Master Potter, you will have nothing to regret. He will make of you a masterpiece, an excellent work of art representing Him in you.

Chapter Six
A NEW BEGINNING

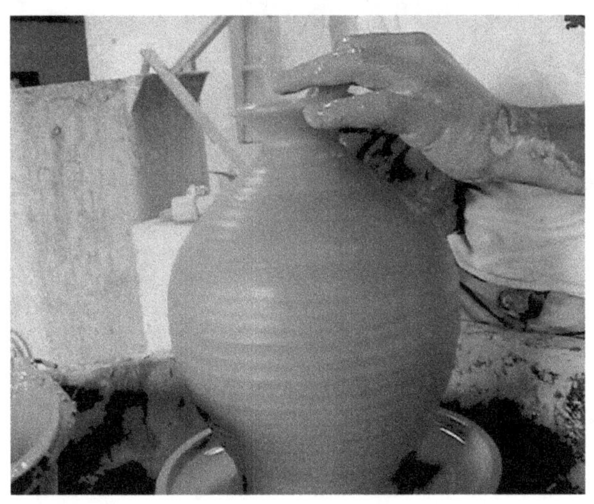

A NEW BEGINNING

**But the pot he was shaping from the clay
was marred in his hands; so the potter
formed it into another pot, shaping it as
seemed best to him.
—Jeremiah 18:4 NIV**

Another unique characteristic of clay is that it can be reshaped. Before firing (the final heat treatment), clay can be kneaded and made into an entirely new shape. No matter how many times it had been used before, and even if it had dried, clay can slake if soaked in water and be used for another vessel or pot. As long as the clay has not been fired, which is the final transformation of the material, there is always hope for it. Until that time, it can be used to produce a better vessel.

That means there is always hope for a man, as long as he is alive. No matter what your past experience may be, God can make you a better vessel. You may have experienced failure and defeat, shame and frustration in the past, but if you can catch the revelation knowledge of what the Lord is saying in Jeremiah 18:4, you need not despair. You are nothing but clay in the hand of God, the Master Potter. Yield your life to Him. Relax under His control and your end will be great. Scripture says:

For a just man falleth seven times, and riseth up again. *(Proverbs 24:16)*

Do not remember the former things, nor consider the things of old. Behold I will do a new thing, now it shall spring forth; shall you not know it? I will even make a road in the wilderness and rivers in the desert. *(Isaiah 43:18-19 NKJV)*

No matter what your past experience may be, God can make you a better vessel.

The Example of Samson

Judges 13 to 16 covers the account of Samson. He was a very special child. His mother's womb had been reserved for Samson's conception. However, as is so often the case, the people around her misunderstood this and said she was barren. She didn't conceive until Samson's birth had been foretold. Then she became pregnant. Because of the special vessel (a Nazarite) this child was going to be, an angel of God instructed Samson's parents about what his mother may or may not do, eat, or drink during her pregnancy, as well as what the baby would be allowed to eat and drink and do after he was born.

The angel of the Lord appeared to her and said, "You are barren and childless, but you are going to become pregnant and give birth to a son. Now see to it that you drink no wine or other fermented drink and that you do not eat anything unclean. You will become pregnant and have a son whose head is never to be touched by a razor because the boy is to be a Nazirite, dedicated to God from the womb. He will take the lead in delivering Israel from the hands of the Philistines." Then the woman went to her husband and told him, "A man of God came to me. He looked like an angel of God, very awesome. I didn't ask him where he came from, and he didn't tell me his name. But he said to me, 'You will become pregnant and have a son. Now then, drink no wine or other fermented drink and do not eat anything unclean, because the boy will be a Nazirite of God from the womb until the day of his death.'" *(Judges 13:3-14 NIV)*

The purpose of Samson's birth was very specifically stated in this chapter too:

"For behold, you shall conceive and bear a son… he shall begin to deliver Israel out of the hand of the Philistines." *(Judges 13:5 NKJV)*

And verse 25 records:

And the Spirit of the Lord began to move upon him. *(Judges 13:25a NKJV)*

The Lord stood by His Word to fulfill it. Samson was a symbol of God's strength to deal with the Philistines. On one occasion, he found a fresh jawbone of a donkey and used it to slaughter a thousand Philistines (Judges 15:15). Samson did great exploits for the Lord with his unusual strength, but eventually, he began to toy with the oil of God on his life. Samson had an eye for the ladies wherever he went, and he went in to them, including prostitutes.

> And Samson went down to Timnah, and saw a woman in Timnah of the daughters of the Philistines. And he came up, and told his father and his mother, and said, I have seen a woman in Timnah of the daughters of the Philistines: now therefore get her for me to wife. *(Judges 14:1-2)*

> Then went Samson to Gaza, and saw there an harlot, and went in unto her…And it came to pass afterward, that he loved a woman in the valley of Sorek, whose name was Delilah. *(Judges 16:1,4)*

Samson began to gamble with women over his destiny but met his Waterloo in Delilah. Note that Delilah was not his wife (Judges 16:4). Read all of Judges 16 to understand the true picture of Samson's reckless immorality.

> Can a man scoop fire into his lap without his clothes being burned? *(Proverbs 6:27 NIV)*

For an anointed man (or woman) of God to join themselves with a strange woman (or man), is an example of self-degradation. If you do that, you lack self-worth and are hurtling toward your own destruction. Cry to God for mercy with dust and ashes over your head to avert His judgment. That is your only hope.

Samson's immorality played into the hands of his enemies. When those enemies captured him, he wanted to display his strength as usual, not knowing the Lord had left him. The Philistines regarded him as a complete weakling because the glory of God had departed from him, and he could no longer overpower them. He ended up like a morsel of bread in their hands. They began to torture him by, first of all, putting out those eyes which he had used to find different women (Judges 16:21). However, when we read the end of Samson's story, we see the God of another chance, the Master Potter at work.

> However, the hair of his head *began to grow again* after it had been shaven. *(Judges 16:22 NKJV, emphasis mine)*

Consider the victory and celebration Samson's recklessness had brought to his enemies before this, as shown in verse 23:

> Now the lords of the Philistines gathered together to offer a great sacrifice to Dagon their god, and to rejoice. And they said: "Our god has delivered into our hands Samson our enemy!" *(Judges 16:23 NKJV)*

What energy do your actions (or inactions) release to the camp of God's enemies? Do they give God pleasure or pain? Job's conduct gave God pleasure. In other words, God was proud of Job.

> And the Lord said unto Satan, Hast thou considered my servant Job, that there is none like him in the earth, a perfect and an upright man, one that feareth God, and escheweth evil? *(Job 1:8)*

Conversely, Samson's conduct was disgraceful to God. It brought Him pain and gave the enemy joy. The Devil received the praise instead of God. In a similar fashion, when we do not do things that bring praise to God, we are giving praise to the Devil. Even so, the Bible says this:

The pot he was shaping from the clay was marred in his hands; so the potter formed it into another pot, shaping it as seemed best to him. (*Jeremiah 18:4 NIV*)

When Samson came to his senses, he remembered God, the One who was able to make Samson into a new vessel again, the Restorer and Sanctifier.

Then Samson called to the Lord, saying, "O Lord God, remember me, I pray! Strengthen me, I pray, just this once, O God!" (*Judges 16:28 NKJV*)

Did the Lord answer him? Yes, He did, but even then, Samson's attitude was not right. Samson reached an ungodly repentance which led him to commit suicide. He said:

"Let me die with the Philistines!" (*Judges 16:30 NKJV*)

May you never die with your enemies in Jesus' name! The Lord restored Samson's strength. If only he had forgotten his past and focused on a new beginning, he may have been another wonder in the land of the living.

The Prodigal Son

Let's take a look at this parable in Luke 15.

Jesus continued: "There was a man who had two sons. The younger one said to his father, 'Father, give me my share of the estate.' So he divided his property between them. Not long after that, the younger son got together all he had, set off for a distant country and there squandered his wealth in wild living. After he had spent everything, there was a severe famine in that whole country, and he began to be in need. So he went and hired himself out to a citizen of that country, who sent him to his fields to feed pigs. He longed to fill his stomach with the pods that the pigs were eating, but no one gave him anything. When he came to his senses, he said, 'How many of my father's hired servants have food to spare, and here I am starving to death! I will set out and go back to my father and say to him: Father, I have sinned against heaven and against you. I am no longer worthy to be called your son; make me like one of your hired servants.' So he got up and went to his father.

"But while he was still a long way off, his father saw him and was filled with compassion for him; he ran to his son, threw his arms around him and kissed him. The son said to him, 'Father, I have sinned against heaven and against you. I am no longer worthy to be called your son.' But the father said to his servants, 'Quick! Bring the best robe and put it on him. Put a ring on his finger and sandals on his feet. Bring the fattened calf and kill it. Let's have a feast and celebrate. For this son of mine was dead and is alive again; he was lost and is found.' So they began to celebrate." *(Luke 15:11-24 NIV)*

Jesus told this story of a lost son. This man had two sons. The youngest persuaded him to divide his property and give him his share. His father yielded to his pressure and gave him his share of the estate. This younger son put together all he had and traveled to a distant country where he wasted everything in riotous living. Not long after his spending spree, a severe famine broke out in that country and the son was hungry. He took up a menial job at a pig farm, and wished he could eat the pig food, but no one even offered it to him. What a pathetic testimony!

However, this story changed "when he came back to his senses" (Luke 15:17). He remembered how comfortable he had been in his father's house. There, even the servants had more than enough to eat. So, he decided to swallow his pride and return to his father and offer himself as a servant. He took a decisive step to return and apologize to his father in repentance. The father's response was unexpected.

> So he got up and went to his father. But while he was still a long way off, his father saw him and was filled with compassion for him; he ran to his son, threw his arms around him and kissed him. *(Luke 15:20 NIV)*

After the young man apologized to his father, his father ordered that he be dressed in a beautiful robe, have a ring put on his finger and good sandals on his feet. A feast was organized in his honor because, according to his father, he was lost but now was found. Within minutes, this young and foolish son that had been destitute, was dressed and being treated as royalty. In the same way, our heavenly Father welcomes us when we return to Him too. He does not count our past sins and mistakes against us, once we have repented. As far as the east is from the west, so far has He taken away our sin. He will remember them no more (See Psalm 103:12 and Isaiah 43:25).

Peter

There was a point in the apostle Peter's life that he denied the Lord, abandoned the ministry, and misled others.

Now Peter was sitting out in the courtyard, and a servant girl came to him. "You also were with Jesus of Galilee," she said. But he denied it before them all. "I don't know what you're talking about," he said. Then he went out to the gateway, where another servant girl saw him and said to the people there, "This fellow was with Jesus of Nazareth." He denied it again, with an oath: "I don't know the man!" After a little while, those standing there went up to Peter and said, "Surely you are one of them; your accent gives you away." Then he began to call down curses, and he swore to them, "I don't know the man!" *(Matthew 26:69-74 NIV)*

Simon Peter, Thomas (also known as Didymus), Nathanael from Cana in Galilee, the sons of Zebedee, and two other disciples were together. "I'm going out to fish," Simon Peter told them, and they said, "We'll go with you." So they went out and got into the boat, but that night they caught nothing. *(John 21:2-3 NIV)*

The same Jesus Peter had denied appeared to him and his friends after His death and resurrection. He performed a miracle for them then too—another miraculous catch of fish.

Early in the morning, Jesus stood on the shore, but the disciples did not realize that it was Jesus. He called out to them, "Friends, haven't you any fish?" "No," they answered. He said, "Throw your net on the right side of the boat and you will find some." When they did, they were unable to haul the net in because of the large number of fish.

Then the disciple whom Jesus loved said to Peter, "It is the Lord!" As soon as Simon Peter heard him say, "It is the Lord," he wrapped his outer garment around him (for he had taken it off) and jumped into the water. The other disciples followed in the boat, towing the net full of fish, for they were not far from shore, about a hundred yards. When they landed, they saw a fire of burning coals there with fish on it, and some bread. Jesus said to them, "Bring some of the fish you have just caught." So Simon Peter climbed back into the boat and dragged the net ashore. It was full of large fish, 153, but even with so many the net was not torn. Jesus said to them, "Come and have breakfast." None of the disciples dared ask him, "Who are you?" They knew it was the Lord. Jesus came, took the bread and gave it to them, and did the same with the fish. *(John 14:4-13 NIV)*

God knows how to handle each and every one of us.

This was Jesus' method of reaching out to Peter. The love of God is truly unfathomable. After denying Jesus, Peter must have felt like a failure. He needed encouragement and reassurance of his Master's love and acceptance. God knows how to handle each and every one of us. He also knows how to attract our attention. Even though Peter had left his first love and calling, Jesus sought him and gave him another chance. Jesus forgave, restored, and redirected him with a clear vision and a direct mandate. Jesus told Peter to do this: "Feed my sheep" (John

21:17). If Jesus did this for Peter, He will do it for us too. Jesus is the same yesterday, today and forever (Hebrews 13:8).

Though your case may be as bad (or even worse) than Peter's, the Lord is reaching out to you in love. Have you denied the faith? Have you lost your first love? Have you soiled the garment of righteousness which the Lord gave you when you got saved? Did you shed blood? Are you divorced? Have you broken faith with your partner? Are you heavily weighed down with guilt? All hope is not lost! Thank God you are still alive. The Master Potter is able to form you into another pot, reshaping you as it seems best to Him. He says this in Matthew:

> "Come unto me, all ye that labour and are heavy laden, and I will give you rest" *(Matthew 11:28)*

And remember that it also says:

> Cannot I do with you as this potter? saith the Lord. Behold, as the clay is in the potter's hand, so are ye in mine hand. *(Jeremiah 18:6)*

We must practice confessing our sin, forgetting the past, and moving forward. The process of introspection and repentance is one we should always employ—even when we think we are doing well. Each day is another day—a new beginning with fresh hope and opportunities. Rehearsing our regrets and failures or basking in our glories will distract us from our true purpose in God for today. It is impossible to advance progressively with our eyes focused on our past, so we need to turn our back on all our failures, achievements, and disappointments, so that we can stay focused and get where God is leading us instead. As the apostle Paul wrote,

Brothers and sisters, I do not consider myself yet to have taken hold of it. But one thing I do: Forgetting what is behind and straining toward what is ahead, I press on toward the goal to win the prize for which God has called me heavenward in Christ Jesus. *(Philippians 3:13-14 NIV)*

We must practice confessing our sin, forgetting the past, and moving forward.

SOVEREIGNTY OF THE MASTER POTTER

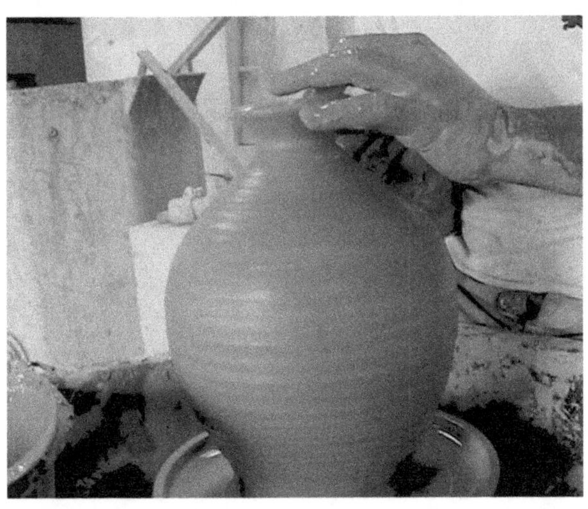

SOVEREIGNTY OF THE MASTER POTTER

God Almighty, the Master Potter, has the greatest power in the whole universe. He is the Lord. He is the Supreme Commander of the armies of heaven and earth. He is the President of all presidents and governs all the governors. His authority cannot be challenged. He is the Creator and Sole Administrator of the whole universe. He controls all His creation—man, animals, plants, the elements—sun, moon, stars, wind, mountains, everything, and He uses everything to fulfill His purposes. The Lord is in charge. He controls thrones and domains in heaven, on earth, and in the waters. Nothing happens without His permission. His power is displayed all over the Bible, and is described as incomparable and great (Ephesians 1:19).

Scriptural Displays of His Sovereignty

In Creation

The Lord Almighty created all things. Genesis 1 tells us that originally the earth was formless and empty. Darkness covered the earth everywhere.

And God said, "Let there be light," and there was light. God saw that the light was good, and he separated the light from the darkness. God called the light "day," and the darkness he called "night." And there was evening, and there was morning–the first day. *(Genesis 1:3-5 NIV)*

This was the beginning of creation. God created the light and everything else by His Word. He called the things that were not into existence by His unquestionable authority. He displayed His awesome power through verbal command. No other god or power has displayed such authority.

> ## The Lord is in charge. He controls thrones and domains in heaven, on earth, and in the waters. Nothing happens without His permission.

Dominion and Worship

The Lord Almighty rules in dominion, and He alone is worthy to be worshiped. In 1 Samuel 5, when the ark of the covenant was captured by the Philistines, they carried it into the temple of their god, Dagon. The people of Ashdod woke up the next day to see that Dagon, their god, had fallen with his face to the ground before the ark of the Lord. They took the idol up and returned him to his place. The following morning, they woke up to discover that Dagon had fallen again with his face on the ground before the ark. Once again Dagon lay prostrate before the ark, but this time his head and hands had been broken off.

The Lord's hand was heavy on the people of Ashdod and its vicinity; he brought devastation on them and afflicted them with tumors. When the people of Ashdod saw what was happening, they said, "The ark of the god of Israel must not stay here with us, because his hand is heavy on us and on Dagon our god." *(1 Samuel 5:6-7 NIV)*

The Lord displayed His dominion over Dagon and made it clear to the people of Ashdod that He alone was worthy to be worshipped.

Supernatural Power

The Lord sent Moses to pharaoh to release His people so they could worship Him. To display His miraculous power, the Lord asked Moses to tell Aaron to throw his staff on the ground. When it turned into a snake, this arrogant ruler thought there was nothing special in this miraculous act, so he called his magicians to do the same. Though his magicians made their staffs turn into snakes, the Aaron's snake swallowed all their snakes in victory.

The Lord said to Moses and Aaron, "When Pharaoh says to you, 'Perform a miracle,' then say to Aaron, 'Take your staff and throw it down before Pharaoh,' and it will become a snake." So Moses and Aaron went to Pharaoh and did just as the Lord commanded. Aaron threw his staff down in front of Pharaoh and his officials, and it became a snake. Pharaoh then summoned wise men and sorcerers, and the Egyptian magicians also did the same things by their secret arts: Each one threw down his staff and it became a snake. But Aaron's staff swallowed up their staffs. *(Exodus 7:8-12 NIV)*

Through this, the Lord proved that His power could not be challenged. At one point, as the Lord rained down the ten plagues on Egypt due to Pharaoh's stubbornness, his magicians exclaimed:

"This is the finger of God." *(Exodus 8:19)*

They were overwhelmed by the power of the Most High God. God mobilized creation in His battle against Pharaoh and Egypt. He used snakes, water, frogs, gnats, flies, boils, hailstorms, locusts, darkness, and death to fight against the enemy of His people. No power can be likened to the power of Jehovah. He is God Almighty.

His Glory

The Bible records this in Psalm 19:

The heavens declare the glory of God; the skies proclaim the work of his hands. *(Psalm 19:1 NIV)*

God Almighty is the King of Glory, and He will not share His glory with any man. In Daniel 4, King Nebuchadnezzar thought he achieved all he had by his own might. He attempted to share God's glory. The Lord humiliated him, took away his senses, and drove him into the bush to eat grass like a beast of the field for seven years until he looked up to heaven and acknowledged God. He finally proclaimed:

At the end of that time, I, Nebuchadnezzar, raised my eyes toward heaven, and my sanity was restored.

Then I praised the Most High; I honored and glorified him who lives forever. His dominion is an eternal dominion; his kingdom endures from generation to generation. *(Daniel 4:34 NIV)*

Then, the Lord restored the king to his position.

Deliverance

In Daniel 3, Shadrach, Meshach and Abednego refused to bow down to the king's golden image because of their faith in the Sovereign God. The king was so furious with them that he commanded they be cast into a fiery furnace. In spite of his threats and persuasion, these young men would not budge in their stand for God. In his wrath, the king asked that the furnace be heated up seven times hotter and that they be cast into it. The furnace was so hot that the flames of fire even killed the soldiers who carried them to the furnace (Daniel 3:22). But God manifested His deliverance power on Shadrach, Meshach and Abednego. They were not burnt. They were not harmed in any way. Their robes were not scorched, and there was not even a smell of the fire on them (verse 27). Instead of just the three young men, King Nebuchadnezzar saw four men in the fire. This means that the Lord Himself came down to be with them in that fire. Finally, the king proclaimed:

"Praise be to the God of Shadrach, Meshach and Abednego…Therefore I decree that the people of any nation or language who say anything against the God of Shadrach, Meshach and Abednego be cut in pieces and their houses be burned into rubble, for no other god can save in this way." *(Daniel 3:28-29 NIV)*

The Lord Almighty possesses the power to kill or make alive. He is the Death of death and hell's destruction. He is the Alpha and Omega. When He blesses, no one can curse. He is the One to be feared by all mortals. The Lord Jesus said:

> "I tell you, my friends, do not be afraid of those who kill the body and after that can do no more. But I will show you whom you should fear: Fear him who, after your body has been killed, has authority to throw you into hell. Yes, I tell you, fear him. *(Luke 12:4-5 NIV)*

His Word

God is not separated from His Word; He is inextricably bound to it instead. He honors His Word above His name. It is infallible. Jesus illustrated the integrity of the Word of God:

> "Heaven and earth will pass away, but My words will by no means pass away." *(Matthew 24:35 NKJV)*

The psalmist also said in Psalm 119:

> For ever, O Lord, thy word is settled in heaven. *(Psalm 119:89)*

The Word of God is final. It is the greatest authority. By the Word, God created the entire universe (John 1:1). From it, nations of the world draw their laws and constitutions. The Word is quick and powerful.

The Lord God Almighty is the Great Artist and Master Potter of all times. He is in absolute control of His creation. As men, when we walk in agreement with His sovereign will, we enjoy peace. He will mobilize forces (creation and circumstances) to work in our favor. When we are positioned where He wants us to be, our success is guaranteed. We will prosper and be in good spiritual, physical, and material health, even when others are complaining and fainting. When others say there's a casting down, we say there's a lifting up (Job 22:29).

> But when we walk according to our own carnal will, we work like elephants and eat like ants.

But when we walk according to our own carnal will, we work like elephants and eat like ants. Under such circumstances, we have little to show for our toil. We face wars and chaos within and without. We fight unnecessary battles. It is, therefore, our responsibility as God's children to seek His face before we make any important decisions concerning our lives, including our career, business, marriage partner, place of residence, and anything else that is important. When we seek and do His will, we can be assured of His peace, deliverance, favor, promotion, or whatever He wants to do for us.

Are you facing any battles right now? Does it seem that the Lord doesn't answer your prayers anymore? Does your life feel stagnant? Does it seem like the promises of God are not manifesting for you? Does it seem like things are moving in the opposite direction of God's promises to you? Are you in that situation because the Lord put you there, or because you put yourself there? The first step to take in addressing these problems is to ask God for direction. You will seek Him and find Him, when you seek Him with all your heart. However, you must be careful to obey when He speaks to you. When you do, you can trust Him.

> If you are willing and obedient, you shall eat the good of the land. *(Isaiah 1:19 NKJV)*

> Thou wilt keep him in perfect peace, whose mind is stayed on thee: because he trusteth in thee. *(Isaiah 26:3)*

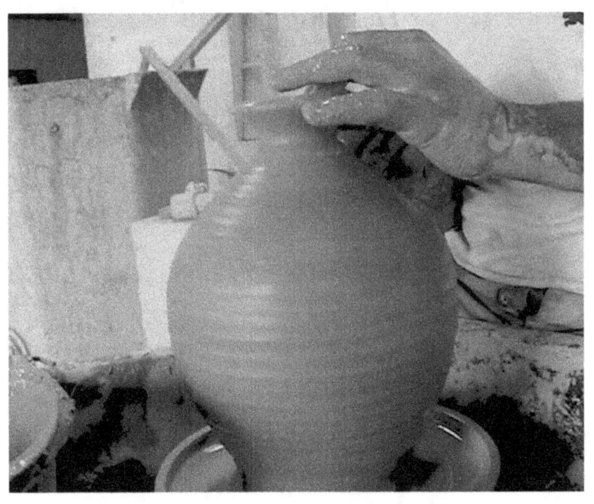

Chapter Eight
INTIMACY WITH GOD

Chapter Eight

INTIMACY WITH GOD

Webster's Dictionary defines intimacy as "a close, familiar, and affectionate personal relationship."[7] This means that intimacy has to do with relationship. It is not just an ordinary relationship, but an affectionate, loving relationship. There can be no intimacy without relationship. Whether we are talking about man or God, we must have a relationship first and foremost. What is relationship? The same dictionary defines that as a connection, association, or involvement. It is an emotional connection between people. To connect is to join, fasten together, or unite; so to have a relationship with God is to be connected or in association with Him. To be intimate with God is to be emotionally joined, fastened together, or united with Him. Can this be described as your position with Him? Are you daily connected to Him? Do you feel any emotion towards God?

> ## There can be no intimacy without relationship.

Knowing about God is one thing, but staying connected to Him is another thing altogether. Being involved in God's service (including being a prayer warrior or Sunday school teacher) is

7. "Intimacy." n.d. Merriam-Webster. Merriam-Webster. Accessed June 23, 2019. https://www.merriam-webster.com/dictionary/intimacy.

one thing, but being connected and in tune with Him is something else entirely. A person can be so occupied with religious activities that he does not have time to commune with God. He does not want to be interrupted by the Owner of the work. Connection has to do with the establishment of a harmonious relationship. Are you doing what you are doing in harmony with the direction of the Holy Spirit and under His divine guidance?

> ## Connection has to do with the establishment of a harmonious relationship.

Intimacy is a higher level of relationship. It is a close and affectionate connection or involvement with God. In this case, the relationship is motivated by a strong feeling of love. Worship and service is not sensual or by eye service, neither is it by compulsion. It is fueled by affection (devotion or love). Intimacy with God is a position, whereby a Christian uncompromisingly and passionately esteems his relationship with God above any other relationship. At this stage, he values or prioritizes God's presence more than anything or anyone else. He is ready to sacrifice anything to be with God and to do His will. This is what is lacking in the body of Christ today. Many would rather give money, take up titles, and prefer to be seen or heard by men, than deny themselves daily to be in their closets and keep their appointments with God.

It is common today to see Christians take on titles as if they determine their spirituality. It is has become the norm to address Christian brothers and sisters as Bishop Tim, Pastor Joe, Evangelist Steve, Apostle Peter, Prophet Simon, and so on. Some people feel seriously offended when addressed without these titles. In fact, to some extent, you can feel out of place or unspiritual these days, if no title is attached to your name. That means you simply don't belong. You don't measure up. You haven't paid your dues. Unfortunately, sometimes we treat others according to this attitude too. The sad truth is that many of these titled brethren hardly spend an hour a day in prayer and study of the Word. They cannot boast of any revelation or message they have personally received from the Lord, and sometimes their sermons are memorized versions of another ministers' teachings. Nevertheless, God is not mocked.

Ministers are identified by the anointing they carry, not the names or titles they bear.

Let us remember that ministers are identified by the anointing they carry, not the names or titles they bear. An apostle, for instance, is not someone who answers to that title and tries to subdue co-workers in God's vineyard. Instead, a true apostle is distinguished from others by his operation in the body of Christ. He works closely with the other fivefold ministers of the gospel. He cares for the body. Paul is a good example of an apostle. He was passionately attached to the church and sincerely desired to see her grow by imparting unto her some spiritual gifts.

> One of the things I always pray for is the opportunity, God willing, to come at last to see you. For I long to visit you so I can bring you some spiritual gift that will help you grow strong in the Lord. When we get together, I want to encourage you in your faith, but I also want to be encouraged by yours. *(Romans 1:10-12 NLT)*

This is what distinguished Paul as an apostle. His works spoke for him. Basically, there is no need for all these accolades unless God asks you to bear them. The purpose of this chapter is not to make us seek the recognition of men by arrogating ministries, accolades, and titles to ourselves, but to stimulate a sincere hunger for a closer walk with God which leads to humility and deeper understanding of who He is instead. We do this by finding our place in the gospel of Jesus Christ and His call upon our lives. Our close and authentic walk with God will speak for itself.

Requirements for Intimacy with God

There are many contributing factors to the development of a deep relationship with God. It requires some effort and sacrifice, especially in self-discipline. Intimacy is cultivated. There is a price to be paid before one can get into God's inner chamber, and it is multidimensional. God is not partial. Anyone who can pay the price can access His presence, but those who do not pay the price cannot be there. It is very simple and straightforward, and it takes time. There are no shortcuts to intimacy with God.

Intimacy is cultivated.

The first step to take in developing a relationship with God is forsaking a life of sin and surrendering one's life totally to Jesus Christ, the Author and Finisher of our faith.

> But as many as received him, to them gave he power
> to become the sons of God, even to them that believe
> on his name. *(John 1:12)*

> For with the heart man believeth unto righteousness;
> and with the mouth confession is made unto
> salvation. *(Romans 10:10)*

This is the starting point. No matter how many years one has been in church, he will have no relationship with God until he takes this step of faith to renounce sin and accept Jesus Christ who died to pay the price for our sin. After giving his life to Christ, there are regular habits a Christian has to engage to help him develop intimacy with God.

Communication with God

Webster's Dictionary defines communication as "the imparting or interchange of thoughts, opinions, feelings, information, or the like by writing, speaking, or signs."[8] To be intimate with God, a Christian should have regular private communication with Him through meditation on the Word of God and prayer (including praise and worship). Just as one cannot be said to have any relationship with somebody to whom he does not speak or listen, one cannot be said to have any relationship with God if he does not communicate with God regularly. There must be private and personal communication going on regularly. Many Christians go to church, get satisfied with listening to other people's interpretation of God's Word and other social interactions, but they do not have personal time with the Lord on their own. They acknowledge Him as *our* Lord, but not as *my* Lord. For some prayer is merely a formality. It might be when they present their "shopping list": "Give me this and do that for me…"

---

8. "Communication." n.d. Merriam-Webster. Merriam-Webster. Accessed June 23, 2019. https://www.merriam-webster.com/dictionary/communication.

The essence of communication is to share thoughts, feelings, and information with the goal of helping the two parties understand each other better. The Lord says that if we draw near to Him, He will draw near to us. Communication with God helps us know His heartbeat, His will, and the direction of the Spirit. Prayer brings us into alignment with His will and positions us to agree with God in submission. Hence, we don't pray to move God to our position; instead prayer moves us to Him and energizes us to pray according to His will:

> "Nevertheless not my will, but thine, be done."
> *(Luke 22:42)*

This is how Jesus prayed in the garden of Gethsemane, and this kind of intimate prayer time is essential for effective service and real spiritual growth.

The Holy Spirit

The Holy Spirit is part of the triune God—God the Father, God the Son, and God the Holy Spirit. He is the Comforter Jesus promised to His followers.

> "And I will pray the Father, and he shall give you another Comforter, that he may abide with you for ever." *(John 14:16)*

When we pray a benediction, we often say:

> The grace of our Lord Jesus Christ, and the love of God, and the communion of the Holy Ghost, be with you all. Amen. *(2 Corinthians 13:14)*

We often ask for the communion or fellowship of the Holy Spirit (or the Holy Ghost). Unfortunately, many Christians never go beyond lip service with t this request, and they never get to know Him personally. The Holy Spirit is our Source of power and vehicle of divine revelation. He enables us to know God. He is the divine Interpreter of God's Word. Without Him, one can hardly understand the Word of God. He also enables us to pray effectively.

> Likewise the Spirit also helpeth our infirmities: for we know not what we should pray for as we ought: but the Spirit itself maketh intercession for us with groanings which cannot be uttered. *(Romans 8:26)*

To develop intimacy with God, a believer needs to desire the infilling of the Holy Spirit. More than that, he needs to commune with Him regularly. Knowing the Holy Spirit is required for us to be able to walk as Jesus did; that's why Jesus called Him the Helper. We must have Him within us if we are to bear fruit in God's service and grow spiritually. The Holy Spirit does a great many, very necessary jobs that enable us to follow God. Without the Holy Spirit, we would be lost. The Holy Spirit convicts us of sin, so we can live holy lives (John 16:8). He leads us into all the truth and helps us understand the Word of God (John 16:13). The Holy Spirit inspires us to desire more of God and pulls us into God's presence for regular divine fellowship. He speaks to us and encourages us to converse intimately with the Father. Worship provokes His presence and opens the door for Him to speak to us. While the believers in Antioch were worshipping the Lord, the Holy Spirit spoke to them:

> While they were worshiping the Lord and fasting, the Holy Spirit said, "Set apart for me Barnabas

and Saul for the work to which I have called them."
(Acts 13:2 NIV)

He does the same today. He desires to speak to us daily, but we need to be available and attentive to Him. He speaks in a still, small voice, and if our lives are too busy doing this and that, we will miss hearing what He has to say to us. Listening to the Holy Spirit is a habit we can form through self-discipline. To hear Him, we must consciously eliminate all the noise, and tune in to His frequency. We can talk to Him as a companion because He is always with us. Only then can we enjoy the fellowship of the Holy Spirit. He is our Counselor.

Fear of God

The fear of God is reverential awe towards God, which gives a man confidence to approach His presence. To be intimate with God, one must live daily in reverence for God. Some Christians pretend to fear God when they are in Christian gatherings, but in private, they behave just like unbelievers. For instance, there are men and women who would not smoke cigarettes openly, but they smoke in secret. They would not want their pastors to know they smoke, but they smoke anyway. They would not want their pastors or some Christians to know they drank alcohol either, so they drink it in secret. This can be true of any area of disobedience. People can practice sexual sin behind closed doors; but in church, they appear holy. In reality, they are hypocrites, living lives of bondage and trying to deceive others about their true condition. But God sees. A man who fears God does not live according to a double standard. He reverences God privately as well as publicly. We can pretend to be zealous and holy, deceiving men, but God cannot be mocked. He knows every man. God sees in secret and in the open.

> The fear of the Lord is a fountain of life, turning a person from the snares of death. *(Proverbs 14:27 NIV)*

To fear God is to hate sin and love righteousness. Through the fear of God, men depart from evil. It is to tremble at His Word to obey it. It is putting God first in everything we do. The fear of God draws a man closer to God, just as sin keeps him away from God.

> Let us hear the conclusion of the whole matter: Fear God, and keep his commandments: for this is the whole duty of man. *(Ecclesiastes 12:13)*

Sacrifice

Sacrifice refers to giving up something you value for the sake of something (or someone) you value even more highly. Sacrifice costs you something. Intimacy with God may involve giving up things too. People commonly do not like to part with their comfort, pleasure, personal time, food, money, and friends. Personal devotion with God may cut one off from some social activities. To spend this time with God, you may have to sleep less; He may direct you to fast too. These are sacrifices. Sacrificing some of these pleasures is essential to spending enough time in God's presence. Doing that shows that we recognize that spending time with God is superior to our sleep or our dinner. We are willing to lay those things down to pursue Him instead. Sometimes it may mean surrendering our personal ambition too, because we cannot have one and also the other. Whatever it takes, it pays to cultivate intimacy with God. The gains are much more than the cost. Following God first is of much greater importance than all else.

For a day in thy courts is better than a thousand.
I had rather be a doorkeeper in the house of my
God, than to dwell in the tents of wickedness.
(Psalm 84:10)

God does not take our sacrifices lightly either. He notes everything we do to follow His will or know Him more. He loves us for that and desires to fellowship with us. He says:

Gather my saints together unto me; those that have
made a covenant with me by sacrifice. *(Psalm 50:5)*

Self-Discipline

Another important factor to the enjoyment of intimacy with God is self-discipline. This refers to the process of training oneself to make good choices with our time and energy. We should be orderly in doing things. Since developing intimacy with God involves time, it requires proper time management and concentration. These are only achieved through disciplining ourselves. This enables us to learn to concentrate, which is vital for meditation. We must learn to employ self-control, a fruit of the Spirit. He orders our lives according to God's priorities, so that our time is redeemed and we reach our potential. To some extent, He gives us some healthy rules to follow, but above all, we are lead to submit to Him through our relationship with Him. Our self-discipline flows out of that, as God is first in our lives.

But seek ye first the kingdom of God, and his
righteousness; and all these things shall be added
unto you. *(Matthew 6:33)*

> See then that ye walk circumspectly, not as fools, but as wise, redeeming the time, because the days are evil. *(Ephesians 5:15-16)*

Noah is a good biblical example of self-discipline. He received instructions for building the ark and carefully executed it to those specification. He took his household and the animals into the ark at the right time, and God locked them in. His exemplary discipline and obedience—probably in the face of some resistance by others around him—saved him and his household and preserved mankind.

> And Noah was six hundred years old when the flood of waters was upon the earth. And Noah went in, and his sons, and his wife, and his sons' wives with him, into the ark, because of the waters of the flood. Of clean beasts, and of beasts that are not clean, and of fowls, and of every thing that creepeth upon the earth, There went in two and two unto Noah into the ark, the male and the female, as God had commanded Noah. And it came to pass after seven days, that the waters of the flood were upon the earth. *(Genesis 7:6-10)*

Righteousness

According to Nelson's Bible Dictionary[9], righteousness is "holy and upright living in accordance with God's standard." It is living a life free of sin and in obedience to God. Righteousness is the character of God. Man was born in sin.

---

9. Bible Dictionary. 2005. Nashville, TN: Thomas Nelson Publishers.

> Behold, I was shapen in iniquity; and in sin did my mother conceive me. *(Psalm 51:5)*

Though man is sinful by nature, righteousness is imputed to him when he accepts Jesus Christ as his Lord and Savior.

> Abraham believed God, and it was imputed unto him for righteousness; and he was called the Friend of God. *(James 2:23)*

When the heart of the Christian turns to God in faith, his sins are forgiven, and God accepts him as His child. However, the believer is expected to build on this foundation by daily walking in purity, integrity, morality, sincerity, trustworthiness, and growing to be like God. The Bible says:

> Wherefore, my beloved, as ye have always obeyed, not as in my presence only, but now much more in my absence, work out your own salvation with fear and trembling. *(Philippians 2:12)*

To live righteously, we have to consciously cut off the old habits and practices that do not align with the Holy Spirit's direction for our lives. This is a prerequisite for communing with God because He is holy, and requires us to live holy too (Leviticus 11:44).

> Lord, who shall abide in thy tabernacle? Who shall dwell in thy holy hill? He that walketh uprightly, and worketh righteousness, and speaketh the truth in his heart. *(Psalm 15:1-2)*

Living in righteousness will not only give access to God's presence, it will also make a man walk in favor with the Lord (Proverbs 14:9).

Consistency or Steadfastness

Consistency describes the process of constantly adhering to the same principles. It is steadfast adherence or holding firmly to what one believes. Intimacy with God requires that a Christian adhere strictly to the abovementioned practices all the time. For instance, one should pray and meditate on the Word of God daily; and if possible, at a given time. It should be a habit, and not happenstance. Daniel was a good example of this. Even when there was a threat to his life, he never missed his appointment (fellowship time) with God.

> Now when Daniel knew that the writing was signed, he went into his house; and his windows being open in his chamber toward Jerusalem, he kneeled upon his knees three times a day, and prayed, and gave thanks before his God, as he did aforetime. *(Daniel 6:10)*

Anna was another example of someone that lived consistently in close fellowship with God.

> And there was one Anna, a prophetess, the daughter of Phanuel, of the tribe of Aser: she was of a great age, and had lived with an husband seven years from her virginity; and she was a widow of about fourscore and four years, which departed not from the temple, but served God with fastings and prayers night and day. And she coming in that instant gave

thanks likewise unto the Lord, and spake of him to all them that looked for redemption in Jerusalem. *(Luke 2:36-38)*

Anna had her own challenges in life, but they never took her away from the presence of God. Everyone knew that she never departed from the temple, which is symbolic of God's presence. She served God with fasting and praying night and day. This meant that abiding in God's presence was her habit. A lot of Christians skip their prayers and Bible study with any flimsy excuse. They miss fellowship so they can run after their own pleasures. Perhaps it is a holiday, or they need more sleep, or they need to cook or they have an appointment with a friend or they are going out with friends or family members. Such people can never have an intimate relationship with God. Intimacy with God requires consistently putting Him first in everything we do. Our private or social engagements should follow our appointments with God, not supersede them.

> **Intimacy with God requires consistently putting Him first in everything we do.**

Mine eyes shall be upon the faithful of the land, that they may dwell with me: he that walketh in a perfect way, he shall serve me. *(Psalm 101:6)*

Humility

And what doth the Lord require of thee, but to do justly, and to love mercy, and to walk humbly with thy God? *(Micah 6:8b)*

> For I say, through the grace given unto me, to every man that is among you, not to think of himself more highly than he ought to think; but to think soberly, according as God hath dealt to every man the measure of faith. *(Romans 12:3)*

> For God resisteth the proud, and giveth grace to the humble. Humble yourselves therefore under the mighty hand of God, that he may exalt you in due time. *(1 Peter 5:5b-6)*

Humility is a necessary requirement to access God's presence. He permits the humble to dwell in the high and lofty place with Him (Isaiah 57:15). Humility is meekness. It is having a modest opinion of one's own position or importance. When we humble ourselves, God will lift us up.

> In your relationships with one another, have the same mindset as Christ Jesus: who, being in very nature God, did not consider equality with God something to be used to his own advantage; rather, he made himself nothing by taking the very nature of a servant, being made in human likeness. And being found in appearance as a man, he humbled himself by becoming obedient to death—even death on a cross! Therefore God exalted him to the highest place and gave him the name that is above every name, that at the name of Jesus every knee should bow, in heaven and on earth and under the earth. *(Philippians 2:5-10 NIV)*

Fellowship with other believers is important, but the time we spend privately developing intimacy with God is much more important. Many Christians are busy running from "pillar to post" to the detriment of their personal relationship with God. Such people are not strong spiritually and cannot stand strong in troubled times. They can only function under a corporate anointing; outside the body of believers they are empty, dry, powerless and vulnerable. The Lord needs to know us as an individual, so we need to take the time to cultivate the habit of meeting Him in personal quiet time. When we add reading and listening to ministers of the gospel to that, we are setting ourselves to grow well. Revelation from sermons and books can enhance your spiritual growth and understanding of the Scripture. However, ministers and their teaching can never take the place of the Bible. You must read the Bible for yourself.

Benefits of Intimacy with God

Understanding

Regular communication between God and man brings about understanding of His thoughts and feelings. Understanding is familiarity with a person. It is a state of cooperation between people, sometimes involving a mutual agreement.

Intimacy helps a man understand God's will, His Word, and His purpose. Understanding refers to the knowledge of God and His ways. It brings about discernment and insight, which is wisdom, and enables man to understand God's timing for different seasons of life and situations. This emanates from constant interaction with God through meditation on His Word and prayer.

> In the first year of his reign I Daniel understood by
> the books the number of the years, whereof the word

of the Lord came to Jeremiah the prophet, that he would accomplish seventy years in the desolations of Jerusalem. And I set my face unto the Lord God, to seek by prayer and supplications, with fasting, and sackcloth, and ashes. *(Daniel 9:2-3)*

Daniel's intimacy with God made him understand that it was the set time for his people's release from captivity, so he started interceding for that purpose. It takes a man of understanding to utilize opportunities as they arise, and key into what God is doing at any given time. Understanding equips a Christian to cooperate with God in the execution of His divine agenda in his life, family, community or church.

Access

Intimacy with God brings about unusual access to Him too. Access makes it easy to reach God and receive answers in prayer.

Draw near to God and He will draw near to you.
(James 4:8 NKJV)

When we draw near to God in intimacy, a person prays and praises God effortlessly with great results. He also hears and receives guidance from God. A good example of this is Joseph (Genesis 40-41) who God used to interpret the dreams of pharaoh's butler and baker because he had access to God. Other examples are Daniel and his friends: Shadrach, Meshach and Abednego. In Daniel 2, King Nebuchadnezzar had a dream which perplexed him and required an interpretation. To make matters worse, he refused to share the dream. He mandated that the magicians, enchanters, sorcerers, and astrologers under him tell the dream and its interpretation, or face execution. This was humanly impossible, so they could not meet the king's demand. These men stood face-to-face with death. This included Daniel too as he was one of the elite leaders under the king too. When they came to get Daniel, he asked for time to seek God. The solution the king demanded was supernatural and Daniel had access to the God who alone could untie the knot to provide the answer. Daniel took the matter to his friends and prayer partners to ask for divine intervention.

> Then Daniel returned to his house and explained the matter to his friends Hananiah, Mishael and Azariah *(These are the Babylonian names of Meshach, Shadrach, and Abednego.)* He urged them to plead for mercy from the God of heaven concerning this mystery, so that he and his friends might not be executed with the rest of the wise men of Babylon. During the night the mystery was revealed to Daniel in a vision. Then Daniel praised the God of heaven… Daniel replied, "No wise man, enchanter, magician or diviner can explain to the king the mystery he has asked about, but there is a God in heaven who reveals mysteries. He has shown King Nebuchadnezzar what will happen in days to come. Your dream and the visions that passed through your mind as you were lying in bed are these." *(Daniel 2:17-19, 27-28 NIV, addition mine)*

God stepped into that situation and everything changed. These four Hebrew young men had probably been brought to Babylon "for such a time as this." God used Daniel and his friends, not just to reveal the dream, but also to bring forth the interpretation and save lives at a critical moment. Through their access to God, they were able to avert a national disaster. God used Daniel to speak to the king and declare His mind to him. Daniel walked out this Scripture in his everyday life:

> "Thy kingdom come. Thy will be done."
> *(Matthew 6:10)*

The access they had to God was like a nutcracker. Their prayer and the answers they received were possible because they lived prayerful and intimate lives with God. If they had not been in the habit of communing with God, they would not have had the courage to turn to Him at this juncture and ask for an answer. Access to God turns problems into opportunities because favor with God commands favor with men. The result was that God was glorified.

> The king said to Daniel, "Surely your God is the God of gods and the Lord of kings and a revealer of mysteries, for you were able to reveal this mystery."
> *(Daniel 2:47 NIV)*

Access to God turns problems into opportunities because favor with God commands favor with men.

Spiritual Gifts

An intimate relationship with God helps a Christian manifest their spiritual gifts. These include word of wisdom, revelation knowledge, prophecy, speaking in tongues, interpretation of tongues, faith, healing, and many others that are outlined in multiple sections of Scripture.

> And God hath set some in the church, first apostles, secondarily prophets, thirdly teachers, after that miracles, then gifts of healings, helps, governments, diversities of tongues. Are all apostles? Are all prophets? Are all teachers? Are all workers of miracles? Have all the gifts of healing? Do all speak with tongues? Do all interpret? *(1Corinthians 12:28-30)*

Nobody can declare God's word (prophesy) beyond the Word of God he knows. Faith also springs out of the indwelling Word of God in a man's life because faith comes by hearing the Word of God (Romans 10:17). Spiritual gifts are developed as a Christian matures and grows in intimacy with God.

Favor from God commands favor from men.

Favor

Pastor Matthew Ashimolowo defined favor as heavenly endorsement, divine approval and the currency of the kingdom of God for the advancement of His work. He further described it as the hand of God that helps a man and God's grace which sustains him. Favor from God commands favor from men. Divine favor made Joseph stand out wherever he was (Genesis 39-40). As a slave in Potiphar's house, the Bible says:

> And his master saw that the Lord was with him, and that the Lord made all that he did to prosper in his hand...the Lord blessed the Egyptian's house

for Joseph's sake;...and he left all that he had in Joseph's hand. *(Genesis 39:3,5-6)*

Daniel and his friends were greatly favored in Babylon, the land of their captivity. Favor is brought about by obedience to God. These Hebrew youth displayed uncommon obedience and dedication to the God of heaven. As a result, God opened the floodgates of heaven upon their lives. While everyone else bowed down to the king's image, they refused to do so, to their own detriment. They preferred roasting in the fire over disobedience to God, but the God of favor followed them *into the fire*, being faithful to His Word that when we pass through the fire, He will be there with us (Daniel 3:16-18). Look at the conclusion of that chapter:

> Therefore I make a decree, that every people, nation, and language, which speak any thing amiss against the God of Shadrach, Meshach, and Abednego, shall be cut in pieces, and their houses shall be made a dunghill: because there is no other God that can deliver after this sort. Then the king promoted Shadrach, Meshach, and Abednego, in the province of Babylon. *(Daniel 3:29-30)*

Divine favor brings promotion, wisdom, uncommon blessings, and a great deal more.

Faith

Faith is unwavering trust in God. It is believing in God's character, who God says He is, and that He can do what He says He can do. It is a confident trust in the truth that God's power is infallible and that He will fulfill His promises even when we have not yet seen the manifestation of them. Hebrews 11:1 describes faith like this:

> Now faith is the substance of things hoped for, the evidence of things not seen. *(Hebrews 11:1)*

Faith is developed and strengthened when we cultivate the attitude of spending time with God, especially as we read His Word. Faith comes by constant studying of the Word of God (Romans 10:17), and is essential for a successful work with God. Faith is the most powerful resource we require to engage God's attention through prayer too.

> But without faith it is impossible to please him: for he that cometh to God must believe that he is, and that he is a rewarder of them that diligently seek him. *(Hebrews 11:6)*

Faith can reverse the natural order of events. By faith we move the hand of God and overturn challenging situations for His glory.

> Elijah was a human being, even as we are. He prayed earnestly that it would not rain, and it did not rain on the land for three and a half years. Again he prayed, and the heavens gave rain, and the earth produced its crops. *(James 5:17-18 NIV)*

This is a very powerful demonstration of faith, an expression of the understanding of the knowledge of the Almighty which comes from an intimate relationship with God. By faith Elijah did amazing exploits for the Lord, made a fool of the Baal worshipers and proved there was no god but Jehovah, the Lord Almighty, the God that answered by fire. Elijah was a man of faith who made his generation acknowledge the God of heaven as incomparable. Let's take a look at the story of the contest between the prophet Elijah and the prophets of Baal. This story is an ideal illustration of faith.

> Then Elijah said to them, "I am the only one of the Lord's prophets left, but Baal has four hundred and fifty prophets. Get two bulls for us. Let Baal's prophets choose one for themselves, and let them cut it into pieces and put it on the wood but not set fire to it. I will prepare the other bull and put it on the wood but not set fire to it. Then you call on the name of your god, and I will call on the name of the Lord. The god who answers by fire–he is God." Then all the people said, "What you say is good." Elijah said to the prophets of Baal, "Choose one of the bulls and prepare it first, since there are so many of you. Call on the name of your god, but do not light the fire." So they took the bull given them and prepared it. Then they called on the name of Baal from morning till noon. "Baal, answer us!" they shouted. But there was no response; no one answered. And they danced around the altar they had made. At noon Elijah began to taunt them. "Shout louder!" he said. "Surely he is a god! Perhaps he is deep in thought, or busy, or traveling. Maybe he is sleeping and must be awakened." So they shouted louder and slashed themselves with swords and spears, as was their custom, until their blood flowed. Midday passed, and they continued their frantic prophesying until the time for the evening sacrifice. But there was no response, no one answered, no one paid attention. Then Elijah said to all the people, "Come here to

me." They came to him, and he repaired the altar of the Lord, which had been torn down. Elijah took twelve stones, one for each of the tribes descended from Jacob, to whom the word of the Lord had come, saying, "Your name shall be Israel." With the stones he built an altar in the name of the Lord, and he dug a trench around it large enough to hold two seahs of seed. He arranged the wood, cut the bull into pieces and laid it on the wood. Then he said to them, "Fill four large jars with water and pour it on the offering and on the wood." "Do it again," he said, and they did it again. "Do it a third time," he ordered, and they did it the third time. The water ran down around the altar and even filled the trench. At the time of sacrifice, the prophet Elijah stepped forward and prayed: "Lord, the God of Abraham, Isaac and Israel, let it be known today that you are God in Israel and that I am your servant and have done all these things at your command. Answer me, Lord, answer me, so these people will know that you, Lord, are God, and that you are turning their hearts back again." Then the fire of the Lord fell and burned up the sacrifice, the wood, the stones and the soil, and also licked up the water in the trench. When all the people saw this, they fell prostrate and cried, "The Lord–he is God! The Lord–he is God!" *(1 Kings 18:22-39 NIV)*

What an awesome God! Faith moves God. This story shows that God is ready and waiting for the opportunity to manifest Himself, but only faith can pull such power down. Elijah's statement: "Let it be known today that you are God in Israel and that I am your servant and have done all these things at your command" shows a strong passion for the glory of God's name as well as exemplary submission. According to Elijah, he did all these things at God's command. Elijah's zeal was to magnify God, not himself. Likewise, when we demonstrate faith, we should do so to draw attention to God, and not to ourselves, so that the unbelieving will see that and surrender to Him. Therefore, faith is a very important tool in evangelism, soul-winning and revival. Oh, that God would raise another Elijah in our generation!

Faith moves God.

Power

The ultimate effect or benefit of intimacy with God is power.

"But ye shall receive power, after that the Holy Ghost is come upon you: and ye shall be witnesses unto me both in Jerusalem, and in all Judea, and in Samaria, and unto the uttermost part of the earth." *(Acts 1:8)*

For the kingdom of God is not in word, but in power. (1 Corinthians 4:20)

Power is the beauty of Christianity. It distinguishes Christianity from other religions. All believers are meant to manifest God's power and do great things for God in their various areas of calling. In fact, all of creation is waiting for this manifestation.

However, this cannot happen until we grow in our intimacy with God. We need to graduate from worshiping at the outer courts, where it is noisy and full of distractions, to getting deeper in the Lord and going into the inner courts where we get totally immersed in the presence of God. The difference between one believer and another (and this includes ministers) is the power they carry. The power they manifest depends on their intimacy with God, which often stems out of the time they spend in God's presence. While some ministers will pray and pray without much impact on the lives of the people, others carry so much power that while they are just sharing the Word of God, demons will be flying out of their captives because the messenger's words carry so much authority. For the latter, so much power is manifested when they are speaking that men break down in tears. Without laying hands on anyone, their listeners are transformed, healed and delivered. Meanwhile, some servants of God shout and dance and perform all manner of gymnastics, yet the lives around them remain unchanged. They are nothing but entertainers. Still others simply rock men to sleep when they are speaking because their words carry no power. Neither of these are walking in the power of God.

> **All believers are meant to manifest God's power and do great things for God in their various areas of calling.**

In Acts 3:1-6, Peter and John met a lame man who asked for alms at the temple gate and healed him. Peter said to him:

> Silver and gold have I none; but such as I have I give thee: In the name of Jesus Christ of Nazareth rise up and walk. *(Acts 3:6)*

This is the kind of power God wants Christians to manifest. Divine power is required to fulfill the Lord's words to his disciples:

> "And greater works than these shall he (you) do; because I go unto my Father." *(John 14:12, addition mine)*

However, there is a price to pay for this to happen. It is the price of drawing nearer to God, to know Him better and have an intimate relationship with Him.

Before You Close This Book

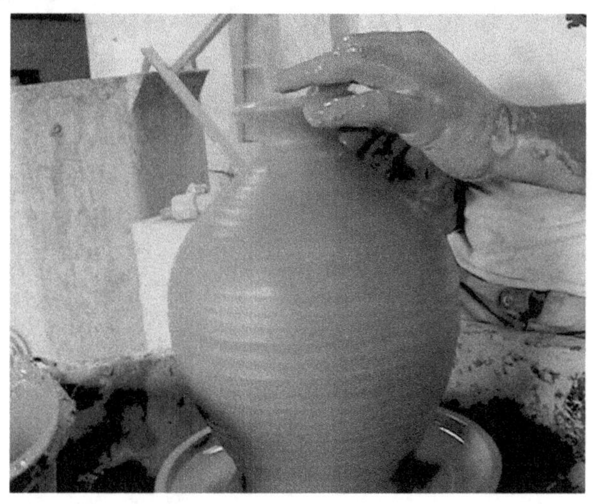

Before You Close This Book

You may not have yet found yourself in the picture painted in this book, especially if you have not surrendered your life to the Lord Jesus Christ. You did not pick up this book by accident. The One who inspired this book, planned that you would come in contact with it, and by this means take a step to receive Jesus into your life. He is the Way, the Truth, and the Life. No man can come to the Father, except by Him (John 14:6). Jesus left His estate in heaven, came down on earth, suffered and died a shameful death on the cross, just to reconcile you to God. Men rarely die for an innocent friend or their own child, but Jesus died for you, a sinner.

Different people have reacted in different ways to this sacrifice of love since then. Some rejected Him; others mocked Him; some denied Him; some betrayed Him; some spat on Him, while still others crucified Him.

> But as many as received Him, to them gave he power to become the sons of God, even to them that believe on his name. *(John 1:12)*

Salvation is the free gift of God. You can't earn it by obeying a set of rules (the law). Jesus paid the price that needed to be paid by shedding His precious blood. You are only required to accept Him by faith. Self-righteousness cannot bring about salvation, so acknowledge your sin and helplessness. Surrender to Jesus Christ. Without faith it is impossible to please God.

There are two destinations for all mortals–hell and heaven. All who do not accept Jesus are destined for hell, a place of eternal torment. However, the ultimate aim of this book is to encourage you to accept Jesus as your Lord and Savior. If you receive Jesus, He will give you the power to be a child of God. When you are a child of God, you will be destined for heaven, a place of eternal joy where there is no sin. This becomes possible, not by your works, but by His grace.

Please say this prayer with me:

> *Lord Jesus, I confess that I am a sinner. Please forgive me of my sins. I accept Your love and open the door of my heart to You. Come into my life. I believe You shed Your precious blood and died to reconcile me to God. Thank You for saving me. In Jesus' name. Amen!*

Congratulations! If you said that prayer from your heart, you just got saved. Now you may go ahead and apply all you have learned in this book. This will help you grow and do well in the Lord. It is also very important that you locate a Bible-believing church near you, and identify with them to worship and serve God.

Shalom!

"Have Thine Own Way, Lord"

Have Thine own way, Lord!
Have Thine own way!
Thou art the Potter, I am the clay.
Mold me and make me after Thy will.
While I am waiting, yielded and still,

Have Thine own way, Lord!
Have Thine own way!
Search me and try me, Master, today!
Whiter than snow, Lord, wash me just now.
As in Thy presence humbly I bow.

Have Thine own way, Lord!

Have Thine own way!
Wounded and weary, help me, I pray!
Power, all power, surely is Thine!
Touch me and heal me, Savior divine.

Have Thine own way, Lord!
Have Thine own way!
Hold o'er my being absolute sway!
Filled with Thy spirit till all shall see
Christ only, always, living in me.[10]

10. Adelaide A. Pollard and George C. Stebbins, "Have Thine Own Way, Lord," Have Thine Own Way, Lord MIDI | Adelaide A. Pollard / George C. Stebbins, accessed June 18, 2019.

Endorsements for *The Master Potter:*

"I have read *The Master Potter* over and over. It is a wonderful spiritual tool for everybody, especially for raising young Christians."

— Ngozi Nnoruka
Retired mechanical engineer, Enugu, Nigeria

"This is a masterpiece! It is flawless and clear. The message is as thought-provoking as it is revealing, reviving, and inspiring. It challenged me personally (as the clay) to depend more on the Master Potter for processing, so I would become better working material. Thanks! I received an all-around ministration from *The Master Potter.*"

— Abigail Okolo
Schoolteacher, Enugu, Nigeria

"*The Master Potter* is a masterpiece. I see it as a timely message from God, not only to professing Christians, but to humanity as a whole. The illustrations are superb, to the point, and highly inspirational. The clarity of expression and the precision of the language are outstanding. Above all, the book challenges the saints of today in a huge way regarding their need to abide in God's presence as well as allow Him to work out His divine purpose for their lives."

— The late Dr. Chioma Uzoho
Until her death, master lecturer in the Department of Modern European Languages, Nnamdi Azikiwe University (UNIZIK), Awka, Nigeria

"*The Master Potter* propelled and parachuted me to a much faster yielding unto the Lord. It was like a 'starter' to my journey of faith."

— Okwuchukwukwuru Okpara, PhD
Health Administration, Missouri, Texas

About the Author

Nwabuogo N.B. Okafo is a wife, mother, gifted writer and motivational speaker. She has a Master's degree in Fine Arts, and was the head of pottery division in the Ceramics Production Department of Projects Development Institute (PRODA), Enugu, Nigeria, a research institute of the Federal Ministry of Science and Technology. She worked with clay for over two decades, an experience God used to teach her about His dealings with man.

She loves and serves the Lord passionately with her family. She is currently a graduate student of Biblical Exposition at Liberty University School of Divinity in Lynchburg Virginia. A firm believer in teamwork, she is also one of the National Coordinators for Women Intercessors for the Church and the Nations (also known as Wailing Women Worldwide USA). She is also passionate about motivating men and women to find their place in Christ through total submission and in-depth study of the Scriptures.